The World of
Jesse Stuart
Selected Poems

SAVE EVERY LAMB
DAUGHTER OF THE LEGEND
MY LAND HAS A VOICE
MR. GALLION'S SCHOOL
COME GENTLE SPRING
COME BACK TO THE FARM
DAWN OF REMEMBERED SPRING
BEYOND DARK HILLS
THE LAND BEYOND THE RIVER
32 VOTES BEFORE BREAKFAST

For Boys and Girls

PENNY'S WORTH OF CHARACTER
THE BEATINEST BOY
RED MULE
THE RIGHTFUL OWNER
ANDY FINDS A WAY
OLD BEN
A RIDE WITH HUEY THE ENGINEER

Woodcut by Woodi Ishmael

The
World of
Jesse Stuart
Selected Poems

by
Jesse Stuart

*Edited and with an Introduction
by J. R. LeMaster*

McGraw-Hill Book Company

*New York   St. Louis   San Francisco
Düsseldorf   London   Mexico   Sydney   Toronto*

Book design by Marcy J. Katz.

123456789 BPBP 798765

Library of Congress Cataloging in Publication Data

Stuart, Jesse, date
     The world of Jesse Stuart.

PS3537.T92516A6 1975   811'.5'2   75-5794
ISBN 0-07-062212-4

Contents

The World as Song Singing Itself

The World as Springtime Kentucky Hills

The World as Ship of State

The World as Journey to Ephesus

The World as Universal Brotherhood

Woodcut by Woodi Ishmael

Introduction

When Jesse Stuart published his humorous novel *Taps for Private Tussie* (New York, 1943), and then followed it with a collection of poems entitled *Album of Destiny* (New York, 1944), he unwittingly defeated his dream of being an American Robert Burns. *Taps* established him as a writer of fiction, and the old bardic tradition of the poet had already died. America had survived World War I, and without a significant sense of accomplishment. The feeling of loss which characterized Victorian England had made its way across the Atlantic, and postwar Americans were rootless, homeless, and generally skeptical about their future. The war had accelerated technology, industrialization, and urbanization. Modern science had staked out its claim on man's future in the form of a knowledge explosion, and efforts were underway to get art off the farm and into the city.

Jesse Stuart began his writing career in that unsettled decade of the twenties, and perhaps with more hindsight than foresight. Out of disgust for their country, many young intellectuals had gone abroad during the war and had searched in desperation for a home away from home, only to find that their rootlessness, their sense of loss, went with them. As Ernest Hemingway discovered, we had killed off the old gods, and there were no new ones to take their places. In nineteenth-century England, Matthew Arnold had conceived of art as a substitute for religion, and in America Walt Whitman had dreamed of a day when the poet would replace the priest. By the twenties, the priest has indeed lost his robes, but they were not passed on to the poet. The post-Christian era had begun, and there would be no turning back. Rather, European utilitarianism would be replaced by Yankee pragmatism, and *Angst* would make its way into our linguistic stock and trade.

Every era is probably a pivotal point located somewhere between the one before it and the one which follows it. There are times, however, which are more pivotal than others in that they contain more of the future in the moment and therefore are marked by greater frustrations. Such was the time during and after the war, a time which lent itself to a national paralysis of such magnitude that we hit bottom in 1929 and consequently began asking questions about what was wrong with America—about what was wrong with modern man.

When they came, the answers to what was wrong were polarized. There were those whose sight was daringly fixed on the future. Ezra Pound was flirting with vorticism and Italian futurism, while T. S. Eliot was reeling under the impact of French symbolists of the nineties. The other extreme, represented in intellectual circles by the Agrarian Movement at Vanderbilt University in the thirties, called for falling back to a pre–Civil War agricultural existence in order to reestablish the American identity with land. There would be no falling back, of course, and the Agrarian Movement would quickly be forgotten. By midcentury it would become an object of ridicule; and in the seventies, with greater distance, presumably accompanied by greater hindsight, we would dismiss the matter by saying that it could only have happened in a depression.

It did happen in a depression and we survived both the depression and the Agrarian Movement, but there have always been those in our midst who have doubted the wisdom of abandoning life on the land in favor of life in the city, of abandoning man's "right relation" to the land, his place in nature. When Jesse Stuart was still young, he began buying up land in Greenup County, Kentucky, and he didn't stop buying it until he owned more than a thousand acres. Over the years he has refused jobs in Los Angeles, New York, Chicago, and other large metropolitan areas. He has consistently refused to leave his farm, which he has jealously guarded against the world without. An untiring conservationist, he has farmed successfully. But, most of all, his farm has been his stay against the chaos and desperate living beyond its border. When one visits Stuart in W-Hollow today, sooner or later one is impressed that one is not in the real world, the world of one's daily existence. And sooner or later one says to oneself, "America could have been like this. America could have been this kind of paradise."

Stuart's farm, of course, reflects more than the way of life he believes in. It also reflects his artistic temperament. Throughout his more than forty years of writing, his farm and its occupants have been his subject matter. In more than thirty-five books of fiction and poetry, he has held his farm before the world as a microcosm of what America could have become, and he laments the fact that it did not. Stuart is a patriot, a zealous lover and defender of his country, but he grieves over our present state of affairs. He grieves over what he sees as moral decay, and over what he has witnessed for many years as a falling off in the quality of existence. He grieves, but he has not given up.

In some ways Stuart should be encouraged, for the sixties proved to be more than a decade of protesting the quality of American life, and a decade of dropping out. There had to be a place for dropouts, and that place was frequently the commune. Now that we are in the middle of the seventies, we can see that the commune was only a stopping place, often resembling a hideaway in the Underground Railroad after the Civil War. Although there are still plenty of communes which serve as refuges for those who want to drop out, the major interest does not lie there. Rather, in place of a superficial waiting station, there is a new and vigorous interest in returning to the land. Newspapers and magazines are doing their usual jobs of record keeping, and their statistics indicate that for the first time in the history of the country America's young people are leaving the metropolitan areas faster than others arrive to take their places. Furthermore, most of them are not moving into communes. They are moving into small towns and onto farms. They are returning to the land. And, even if economic necessity partially accounts for the present migration, there seems to be a genuine interest in returning to roots, in restoring man to his old occupation of keeping the flock and cultivating the soil. Either way, Stuart should be pleased.

When the W-Hollow poet published *Taps for Private Tussie* in 1943, it made him a successful fiction writer, in spite of his great ambition to be a noteworthy poet. Up to that time, his reputation as a poet rested heavily upon *Man with a Bull-Tongue Plow* (New York, 1934), which is a celebration of man as "bronzed figure" of the earth. In an effort to arrest his declining reputation as a poet, and at the same time not fully realizing that it was being displaced by his growing reputation as a fiction writer, he published *Album of Destiny* in 1944. He knew that the decade of the thirties had seen the working out of a death struggle between two very different philosophies concerning poetry. Lindsay and Sandburg, as wandering minstrels, were holdovers from an earlier day. Singing about the land, they were the last of the great tradition of poet as bard. In his early autobiography, entitled *Beyond Dark Hills* (New York, McGraw-Hill, 1938), Stuart chastises Sandburg for singing about steelmills:

I am reading your books because I work in steel now. I know you have never worked in steel. If you have worked there, you had a snap. Carl Sandburg, you don't know anything about steel. You got your ideas from walking around the mills at night or talking to the Mayor of Gary, Indiana. Go on and write your excellent poems about the wheat fields and the sunflowers in the wind and the great open spaces of the sundown west, but, Carl Sandburg, lay off writing about steel. Don't disillusion people about the beauty of steel and about the steel birdman that drones and drones in the blue, blue sky. And whatever you do, quit singing about the beauty of steel.

Stuart's paradoxical situation is defined in his chastising of Sandburg. Philosophically he was committed to an agrarian way of life, and consequently to continuing the old bardic approach to poetry. At the same time he could see in Sandburg's writing about steelmills that the bardic approach was dying out. Such people as Eliot and Pound were calling for highly crafted intellectual poetry, and their calls were being heard. Modern man in America, industrialized and commercialized, would live a life which required new forms—and notwithstanding new approaches to art. Conscious of this, Stuart worked for a compromise in *Album of Destiny*. He kept his old subject matter but tried to refine his technique. *Album of Destiny* became his experiment in symbolism, but it attracted little attention. Since the advent of *Album of Destiny* his reputation as fiction writer has continued to grow, although his poetry has been largely overlooked.

The World of Jesse Stuart avoids the usual organization

by chronology, or by so-called "periods of develop-
ment" in the life of the poet. It recognizes, on the other
hand, that the poet's art is a record of his journey
through life. In Stuart's case, the poetry is part of a
larger chronicle, and should be examined not so much
for the real or imagined details of one day at a time or
of one experience at a time. Instead, it is best to look at
the poetry from a distance. When this is done, one
observes that the journey of the poet is through both
time and space, and that the latter is every bit as impor-
tant as the former. Further, in journeying through
space the poet is always in the process of making and
breaking relationships, and this means that he is con-
stantly having to define himself. Every new relation-
ship brings about a death of the old self and at the same
time a birth of the new. In short, the man who drives
cattle over the hill at sunset today is not the same man
who will drive his car into town tomorrow. He takes his
experience of the cattle into the car with him, and the
three of them—man, cattle, and car—drive into town
together in the form of a man who has become a
cattle-man, and a cattle-man who has become a car-
man. The fact that he became a cattle-man first, and a
car-man second, is of utmost importance, for it is the
relationship which defines him. The old relationship,
that of cattle and man, is brought into a new relation-
ship, that of cattle-man and car. Thus the process
continues, and the poet is a fluid self keeping a record
of his ever-changing identity. As an examination of the
poems in this collection will bear out, Stuart's relation-
ships are to be found in both life and death, for,

thought of together, they constitute the ultimate in relationship, the apex of all living as well as of all dying.

The World of Jesse Stuart is organized according to progressive relationships. In the first part the poet is the world. The poems, consequently, are reminiscent of Whitman in that they are primarily about the self. In keeping with the journey as motif throughout Stuart's poems, the first part is more about the one who journeys than about the journey. This is important to Stuart—i.e., this idea of self-examination. It is also important to establishing meaningful relationships. Stuart often repeats Socrates' maxim concerning knowing oneself and continues with observations about being true to oneself. The success of the journey within is essential to the success of the journey without:

> This less-known part of earth is my beginning,
> Heaped high against the wind in little cones;
> I know its soft spring growth and autumn thinning,
> For this dirt is my flesh and rocks my bones.·
> Fresh-water springs that feed the tumbling streams
> With crystal waters are blood from my heart,
> And flow into the outer world of dreams,
> Though my beginning is where these streams start.

Having defined relationships within in terms of correspondences to those existing without, the poet shifts his attention and begins his journey outward through time and space. In the book's second division he examines life as it exists around him on his farm, the relationships which momentarily appear to be outside him, and he immediately identifies with what he sees.

In a Whitmanesque way the "influx of the first part gives way to "efflux," and the poet has found his place in the flux of all being. That such is the case is particularly evident in two of the longer poems entitled "Shinglemill Symphony" and "O What a Poem I Am In."

The poet next journeys through Kentucky (the third division) examining and creating relationships, and then throughout Appalachia (the fourth part). He next journeys throughout America (the fifth part), scattering barbs of satire in protest of what he sees as decadence and cheap living. But national boundaries cannot contain him. In the sixth division of the book he journeys abroad. Passing through one country at a time he makes observations about art, history, culture, and religion. Finally, having escaped national and international boundaries, the poet journeys into the universe (the seventh division) in search of a brotherhood which encompasses all of mankind. When he finds universal harmony, he discovers that it has always existed on his farm in W-Hollow—in the cycle of the seasons, in the flowing of streams, in the blowing of the wind, in life and death as the ultimate relationship.

In as much as Stuart's farm stands as a model for what America could have become, the characters in his poetry and his fiction are types of humanity. Therefore, whether they are modeled after real people or not is largely beside the point. The poet creates them and sustains them in order to stage not the life of a single man who happens to live in Appalachia, but rather the lives of all men. Thus, the journey of the poet, who frequently writes in first person and assumes the role of story teller or of voice in the poem, is the journey of Everyman. Life is a "gauntlet" for all of us. Even when Stuart went abroad, he took his agrarian vision with him. In Egypt, Iran, Greece, Africa, and other countries he looked for character in those people who were most immediately attached to the land. He also looked into the past, to an existence before the advent of modern man. There, in foreign countries too, he looked for quality, and there likewise he failed to locate it in modernity.

When one grants Stuart his subject matter, one experiences little difficulty with the poet's technique. In art as well as life Stuart is given to creating order, and, because of this, throughout his career he has cultivated the sonnet as form. The sonnet is lyrical form, and Stuart has written some of the best lyrics in twentieth-century American poetry; a number of these are to be found in *The World of Jesse Stuart*. On the other hand, the opposite of order is disorder, and one finds as a result that the satires on American life are often close to prose. Most of the poems, however, fall somewhere between superb lyric and flat prose. For example, many of the poet's longer poems are very lyrical because of his mastery of reiterative devices and grammatical parallels. All in all, *The World of Jesse Stuart* should demonstrate that Stuart as craftsman has considerable range. He has strayed far from his youthful dream of becoming an American Robert Burns, but he has remained a poet with unquestionable purpose.

J. R. LeMaster

The World
as Self-Singing

BEGINNING

This less-known part of earth is my beginning,
Heaped high against the wind in little cones;
I know its soft spring growth and autumn thinning,
For this dirt is my flesh and rocks my bones.
Fresh-water springs that feed the tumbling streams
With crystal waters are blood from my heart,
And flow into the outer world of dreams,
Though my beginning is where these streams start.
The land is, too, the foxes' sure domain,
The sedge wherein to hide for dream and sleep;
But for their home, the fortress rock-cliff den,
They have secured themselves a world to keep.
And like the fox I climb to face the wind
Up cone-shaped hills where topmost white oaks are;
I face the morning sun and I don't mind
To face the midnight beauty of a star.

DON'T COME TO SEE ME

While resurrection rises from the ground
With living things that run and fly and crawl
And lucid chlorophyll that helps feed all,
Don't come to see me then; I can't be found.
I can't be kept down with the human fold
When my mind is a wild-bee-tree of dreams
And water has turned silver in my streams,
And field stones on my slopes have turned to gold.
There will not come another time like this
Until this resurrection comes again
When earth is thunder-jarred and spiked with rain.
Don't come: I'll be where resurrection is,
Where torrents from young April spring clouds flood,
Where thoughts soar from the earth to depths of sky,
Where love is higher than the sky is high.
Don't come: I'm wild in my young April mood!

SONG FOR THE NEW YEAR

Hard knuckles of the wind knock on my door.
The clock strikes twelve.
     Another year has ended.
I stop my work with papers on the floor
And put away the books that have befriended
Me on this evening before the fire.
Time at my heels has never brought me fears.
Someday, Time will catch me.
     I shall retire
Since mortal flesh cannot outlast the years.

Time cannot make me tremble like the leaf
When I look at the empty nights and stare;
Midnight is lonely and is filled with grief.
Out there tonight are ghosts of yesteryear.
High in the midnight sky the bright stars glisten
While I begin my New Year with a song,
A melody to make the people listen!
It will be positive.
     It will be strong.

REDEDICATION

April this year will make me fifty-eight,
To see the Aprils here and other places,
To see them bring light to our older faces,
Before Life's ultimatum and the Gate.
No fewer than ten times upon this earth
Had I passed through the Gate and closed my eyes
Never to know again the great surprise,
The hurt of April's haunting me since birth.
Stirred like the sleeping snake by soft spring rain
I rise like water in the April streams,
And like the chlorophyll in cold plant stems,
April, I dedicate myself again.
Time now to execute a higher plan,
To let my mind search higher than a star,
To reach up higher where the unknowns are,
To free myself from decadence of man.

MY HEALTH IS BETTER IN NOVEMBER

Beginning new life on this youthful, splendid day,
November First Nineteen Hundred Seventy-Three.
Leaving St. Joseph's Hospital in Lexington,
Where doctors recommend no heart surgery
But gave a substitute of newer medication,
Two months of slow and low-keyed living at our home.
Dressed in man-clothes I walked to the front hospital
    door
Where our familiar car was parked and where we
    loaded
Hospital possessions and my clothes and radio,
Boxes of get-well cards, letters, and telegrams,
And pots of green-growing and autumn-colored
    flowers.

With legs now less accustomed to my daily walking,
Too long had lain and stiffened on a narrow bed,
My narrow bed with iron rails to hold me on . . .
How exciting to get into our car again,
A bigger radio and twenty classic tapes.
Our farewells to three nurses. Naomi at the wheel,
We moved too slowly from St. Joseph's on our way
To Interstate New Sixty-Four, Direction East,
Toward a morning sunburst rising over hills,
Bluegrass hills shaped like spinning tops and loaves of
    bread.

Now, through the city traffic, red lights and green,
Stops and goes of morning and remembered day.

Sky, indigo-blue bowl, the headdress over earth,
High-blue and arching up and over Autumn's World.
Bright splintered sun so far away and yet was here,
Splashing light fingers on old faded pasture fields.
And limestone rocks like sleeping sheep dotting the
    land,
With herds of pretty cattle, all important breeds.
And horses free to roam in these divided fields,
Separated by wire and painted white board fences.
Reaching superior highway Interstate Sixty-Four
And splitting through sun-tanned wind at eighty-five.
Yes, going home on this magnificent, rare day.
Yes, going home to music of Beethoven on tape.

Away from doctors, nurses, and electrocardiograms.
Away from blood tests, needles, and intensive care.
From odors of hospitals that can't be prevented.
Rolling toward the East, twenty beyond speed limit,
Unmindful of a fine to pay if apprehended;
Not any fine too much to slow our hurrying home
To better living, freedom, laundered breathing air.
On either side our native hills are looming high,
November's multicolored leaves against the sky.
The sourwood, sumac, dogwood, sweetgum, oak and
    pine;
The poplar, sycamore, sassafras, wild grapevine.
This land infertile grows good timber, vegetation;
This land too beautiful for eyes in its four seasons;
My land, beautiful land in autumn's coloring,

With favorite Beethoven music and free of death.
Naomi's speeding through this autumn wonderland,
East Kentucky, United States of America.
Excitement in my brain as we keep going, going,
Riding in comfort, speed, splendor, and homeward
    going.

The thoughts of places I had been were now
        returning,
In other sceneries in other lands I'd known;
Connected with friends long embedded in my brain,
Two thousand or twenty-five hundred years before,
Who left their lives upon the world's poetic pages.

Did Horace remember some November First
Upon the farm where he was born in Venusia?
Any November First, Sixty-five to Eight B.C.?
Did Horace remember the Roman chestnut trees?
The umbrella pines? The cottonwoods and willows?
At fifty-seven his life was too short to be taken.
Did he remember trees, flowers and vegetation,
And fields of grain in harvest on his Sabine farm?
Did he remember November brown with autumn's
        turning
With little freeze and frost on his beloved land?

And Virgil, delightful, gentle, certainly great,
Riding in a chariot from Brundisium to Rome
Along the scenic wonders of his Appian way,

Riding from the seaport Brundisium, great in Virgil's
    day,
In a chariot then back from Rome to Brundisium
Where ships departed for the Mediterranean world—
Did poet Virgil see the turning of the autumn leaves?
Did Virgil carry a notebook taking Latin notes?
Poetic thoughts that stirred his imaginative mind?
Could we but talk to Virgil in this timely hour
About his life from Seventy to Nineteen B.C.
Virgil allotted little time, so how could he
Record his heritage for millennia of posterity,
A heritage that covers now the entire world?

Speaking of allocated time to Roman poets,
About a little regionalist, Valerius Catullus,
Born Eighty-four B.C. departed Fifty-four B.C.
Valerius Catullus has always been with me.
What were Novembers to him in his native Rome?
Thirty Novembers were his allocated time.
Did he observe the willows on the Tiber's banks
In Roman suns and winds two thousand years ago?
Were there sun burnings and November color
    turnings?
But Rome's young regionalist, Catullus, catalogued
His colorful hometown city in his day and time,
Recording turbulence among his friends in Rome.
Two thousand years ago he spoke for us today—
America in Nineteen Seventy-three,
Turbulent and wilder than Catullus' Rome.

But what about Catullus' brief few Novembers?
Were they as pale as Rome's frost-bitten willow leaves?
A cottonwood leaf blowing in a Roman wind
On Tiber banks meandering through eternal Rome?

And what about Simonides with eighty-eight
    Novembers?
Five Hundred Fifty-six to Four Hundred Sixty-eight
    B.C.?
Fifty-six prizes he won in his day and time,
This sweet-voiced sentimental trumpeter of song.
"O stranger, report to the Spartans
That here we lie,
Obeying their commands."
What were Novembers like in Simonides' Athens
Twenty-five hundred years ago in native Greece?
Twenty-five hundred years from then until now
Is long-paced yellowing with passing, passing time;
As thin as vapor thinning on the bluest air
Above the Mediterranean, a world within a world;
The cleanest, bluest air people have ever known.
The Simonides' Athens November was a dream
    month,
A green, blue month, no autumn turning and sun-
    burning.
Did Simonides write "Epitaph for Spartan Dead"
On one of his eighty-eight November Firsts?

One who has stood and watched Greeks plow the
    Theban Plains

In Springtime Nineteen Hundred Sixty-six A.D.,
One who has stood and fondled stones from Pindar's
    home,
Fieldstones piled high where Pindar lived in his
    beloved Thebes.
Here Pindar's lifespan was eighty poetic Novembers.
Five Hundred Eighteen to Four Hundred Thirty-eight
    B.C.
To walk upon this sacred land, turn back the years
Through pages which run into books, encyclopedias.
All this remains where Pindar lived in creativity.
This day, November First, Four Hundred Ninety-six
    B.C.
Did Pindar write a poem in his stone house in Thebes?
How do we know?
        We don't.
                We can surmise and dream.
Back through Time's pages, book, and her
    encyclopedias.
Is there one to dispute when in another world,
Eastern Kentucky, United States of America,
A land unknown in Pindar's Golden Age of Greece,
A land where another poet's life is tied to Pindar,
A time remote, invisible, that keeps the brain
Inactive to receive what has or has not been,
Eighty November Firsts that, maybe, turned and
    burned
In Thebes up North, in the Golden Age of Pindar's
    Greece?

But everywhere there is a serious mood in Greece,
From clean winds wailing over this historic land,
From sea and gulf waves slashing on the rocky shores.
How often have I stood and listened to these songs
The Ancients heard and loved five thousand years
     ago—
The moods of winds and waters and their cypress
     trees,
The tree that stands a vigil for their lonely dead,
That marks their enriched resignations on this land
In little churchyards or where ancient cities stood,
Never a flame of autumn as in this Christmas green.
Greek poets through the centuries observed this tree,
Observed the olive trees in cultivated rows
And growing wild in forests on high mountain slopes.
More olives here than in all countries of the world.
Their leafy branches in the wind and sun are like
Tormented wind-waves on the Mediterranean Sea.
There is sun silvery on upturned leaves and waves;
Their ever-constant motion is pursuing the wind.
There is no golden autumn here but there is mood;
Simonides and Pindar knew this long ago.

Sappho of Mytilene or Eros in Lesbos.
Who knows or cares the dates of Sappho's birth and
     death?
And where in Greece her enriched resignations lie?
We know she was contemporary with Alcaeus.
We know she was a woman poet for women poets,

And she is dateless in literary history.
She did nine thousand lines of poetry in her day
And nine important books, and five of these are lost.
Sappho, a spirit of Earth's literary ages—
Somewhere back in the past on a brisk November First
Sappho wrote an important lyric on this date.
If Sappho could speak out she could tell us which one
And she could tell how cool and comfortable to her
Were those Novembers in the land of legend and her
    birth.

Superior highway ends. We follow State Route One,
A two-lane winding road along the Little Sandy,
A river to compare with Catullus' Tiber;
Our Little Sandy with its willows, cottonwood, and
    birch,
Now with leaves turning, burning in November sun.
This is the road that leads us to our valley home
Where greenest of green meadows carpet valley, hill;
Where multicolored leaves on hills beside the
    meadows
Are turning and November's burning, turning,
    burning,
Sending in each windgust multicolored leaf-drop rain.

Reaching our Valley Farm, this place of earth,
The place I welcome and receive with open arms,
Giving me birth, a body of prolific clay.
This is my Sabine Farm, my Rome, Brundisium,

My Athens, Mytilene, and Thebes rolled into one.
November First Nineteen Hundred Seventy-three.
Invisible hands extending from my house greet me.
Since birth I've been part of this immortal land.
By being part of land I'm brother to the tree,
Returning to my own eternal destiny.

MY HERO

In youth I dreamed that I would lead
Armies like Alexander the Great.
He was my hero when I read
His daring exploits, head of State

Who conquered earth at thirty-three.
My hero since is one who gave
Life to save life at thirty-three,
With hands and feet spiked to a tree.

I WANT TO LIVE

God-given power I go on,
And honest in my travail here,
This spot of earth I have lived on.
And words I've said some men will hear
To make earth better since I've lived,
Protect the earth, help human kin,
Lift up, lift up, because I've lived,
Erase, erase, our human sin.

What profits one to own more than
His share of earth I would not have.
I want to live a friend to man,
Because too soon will be the grave.

LIFE IS A GAUNTLET

How good is life with music and the dream,
With active heart that keeps my body free
And pumps the body's blood in constant stream,
That activates my brain's creativity.
Across Kentucky's April world we drive
Where there's no other beauty to compare;
A resurrected springtime world alive
With golden meadows stirred by clean, cool air.
A birdhawk gliding on his small wingspread,
With beady eyes he searches grass below;
Famished for food, preparing for his kill,
He dives, directed by the way winds blow,
Then rises with a field mouse in his bill.
Out in this mystic world while April's here,
I am alive rejoicing on my earth
In swimming time that knows no death and bier.
Life is a gauntlet I have run since birth.

PROCLAIMED AMBITION

This night of mine has not been spent in splendor
For this has been a night of loneliness,
While here alone the fire has died to ember;
This day has been spent in creativeness.

How can I ever reach the splendid stars
In my ambition for the highest aim?
Stretch my hands up to Jupiter and Mars,
Heights that my world ambition would proclaim?

My mind and heart have soared beyond my reach;
I can't control excited mind and heart.
I am a little teacher here to teach;
I am world citizen to do my part.

THE UNIVERSAL PLAN

I am not regionalist
But I am universal;
It's taken me long to learn
And know of man's survival.

It's taken me these years
To know with trial and practice;
With argumentative man,
The universal plan.

To be man civilized
On earth in my life span;
I have no right to kill,
Another's blood to spill.

No one on earth can make me
Take a life, I've concluded;
Because I can accept death
Before I'm forced to this.

A world to come, nonkilling,
I hope I do not miss;
I'll never know. I'll be gone.
I pray for man's new dawn.

TO BE WITH YOU

I long to be with you when white percoon
Is flower carpets on Kentucky hills,
To be with you beneath a fickle moon
When young night winds are hugging daffodils.
I long to be with you when lilting leaves
Muffle the morning songs we like to hear,
When swarms of multicolored butterflies
Breakfast on blossoms in the honeyed air.
To live with you through ecstasy of spring,
To walk with you under the leaf and vine,
To hear love songs the parent redbirds sing,
Beside their love-nest hidden in the thyme.
Together we can stand upon this land
Where birds rejoice in song in every cove,
United in our hearts as hand in hand
We go to meet our springtime world we love.

WHEN SPRING RETURNS

When spring returns across the empty hollows
And blows his breath among Kentucky hills,
I'll find you here among the loamy sallows,
Among the sweet white-throated daffodils.
When spring returns to mountain glen and rocks
I know that I'll be able to discern
You there among the slender blooming phlox,
You there among the wild green-latticed fern,
Where good rich earth from rotted railfence lingers.
I'll stop, Naomi Deane, to see you twice
Among the neatly pattern'd lady's-fingers,
You there among blue-blooming beggar-lice.
I shall see you in wild white trillium
A-growing by a mountain river stone;
I shall see you reflected in that stream—
And seeing you I shall not be alone.

TWO LEAVES

The multicolored hosts drift down the sky,
Hand-heart-star-shaped and autumn-light and thin,
And you and I are two leaves drifting by
With other loves in legions of the wind.
Look up, my love; don't turn your head away.
Look high, my love, as if you were a star.
You are the golden leaf; I am the gray.
And we go drifting as the others are.
Come, put your hand in mine; let's not pretend.
For love is just as high as we are high.
We'll travel on the silver lanes of wind
Among the other lovers in the sky.

REST NOW, YOUNG BRAIN

Rest now, young brain, for dreams will break too soon
And shatter on your world like slivered glass.
These dreams will be as mists beneath the moon
And lonely as winds muffling autumn grass.
I speak to you of dreams since I've known dreams
And blood that flows in you has flowed in me.
I warn you dreams are only flower stems
And sap that comes each season with the tree.
Rest now, for you have years of life to face
And many paths to walk beneath the sun.
You'll know the joy and sting of love's embrace
Before your travail on this earth is done.
Rest now, young brain, in tender brittle growth!
Be still, small hands; do not clutch for the wind!
Rest now, for many dreams will come with youth!
Be frugal with the life you have to spend.

IF YOU SHOULD PASS

I cannot sing forever like spring grass
For you when passion in this brain is done.
I'll die much quicker than the wind in grass,
My words be darkened like the noonday sun,
Obscured by mountains of dark rolling cloud.
I cannot sing forever like the wind,
Naomi Deane; the wind for you sings loud
And soft, sweet music of the violin.
But I can sing for you this timely hour
While white heat deeply stirs this mortal brain;
Sing songs as fragile as a woodland flower,
And sing and sing while powers of life remain.
If you should pass, eternity-faithful friend,
If you should pass, I fear this song would end.

ARISE, MY LOVE

Arise, my Love! Arise and go with me!
Get up from this soft bed! Throw back the cover!
Look at the big full moon, fringed by a tree!
See clouds like small white ships go sailing over!
Our greening hills rest quietly in sleep;
So come now while the moon is bright and high!
Come on, this is the time for us to keep
Vigil with brilliant moon, white cloud, blue sky.
We loved such lush nights in our youthful prime
For our small world was then and is still a dream.
Each soft night wind still blows a perfect rhyme;
A wild rose blossoms from each briary stem.
You know, my Love, the present is the best!
Live while we can for time will surely pass!
Let us love this night more than all the rest
So we can leave our shadows on the grass.

WE SHALL NOT LIE TOGETHER
IN THE TOMB

We shall not lie together in the tomb
For there will be a wall to separate
Us in finality, and in each room
The husks of what we were won't contemplate
The joy of kiss and touch beyond recall.
How can your sweet voice then communicate
When music will be muffled by the wall
Where you and I will be sealed to our fate?
I cannot hold you close nor touch your hand.
Nor will our lips thrill to the magic kiss
On our pine boards beneath the clayey land.
Why should all lovers have to come to this?
But when we entered life we came alone.
Departing now we go divided ways.
My Dear, when you and I become the gone
I hope I can forever sing your praise.

TOO MANY ROADS

We stand here idle, half afraid to stir.
We cannot even find the path to take.
Too many roads are leading everywhere,
Through pasture field, cornfields, and brushy brake.
Here are the skies, the good clean wind to breathe,
The deep rich loamy earth beneath our feet;
And here are many roads to take or leave,
Earth for the bed, the clean wind for a sheet.
It does not matter much the way we go,
Or where we go, or when, or how, or why.
For we must keep our feet upon the earth
And we must live in wind beneath the sky.
The road lies here before us; if I lose
It is my fault. No certain road I choose.

PATTERNS

Come, Love; let us resign ourselves to patterns
We did not make, patterns we do not choose.
The ancient gods did strangely cut these patterns,
That you and I, my Love, must finally lose.
Remember, spring, my Love, was our beginning,
And summer, Love, we did experience growing.
Remember, spring for us was love and mating,
Autumn for us and we are dead leaves blowing.
Autumn has nipped the growth of us like frost.
We stand here barren trees in fading dawn.
Leaves have flown down; our little paths are lost.
Shall we soon be ghost patterns journeying on?
Patterns we choose would be youth found forever!
There would not be this resignation either!

I WILL TURN FROM THE SOUND OF THE JET

I will turn from the sound of the jet
High in the heavens that I cannot see,
Carrying from one to three hundred passengers
To large cities of my country
And to great cities over the world.

Why should I stand to listen to this familiar sound?
Why should I stand and wonder who is riding
On the jet that I shall never see?

But tonight when the full moon is high
I shall listen to the poetry
Of the wind in the August leaves.
Tonight when the moon is very high
And the wind is there among the leaves
I will read poetry and I shall have music
More Beethoven than the lonely barking of a fox.

WHY SHED TEARS?

I've gone as far as I can in this wood
Where our fence wires are middle of the trees.
Prevented by old illness or I would
See more of old familiar haunts than these.
My father's land I worked at seventeen.
Now I've returned to see old fields and fences.
I can't forget the early springtime green,
Here where I used to study Latin tenses
When I went to the pasture for the cows.
I used to take my youthful time to think
When I sat by to watch the cattle browse.
In early years I used the oakball ink
To scribble lines upon the clean white page.
This struggle's gone into oblivion.
I am considered poet now and sage,
After my better years of life are gone.
I have returned to haunts to meditate,
To see beginnings of formative years,
To see beginnings of my early fate.
Crude though they were, I shed no tears.

NIGHT SONG

Not with my hands can I push night away,
Nor can I lift these formless quilts of night
That blanket earth in stilly-dark array
And fade when morning ushers in new light.
Often I wonder when the day is gone,
When tree and hill are lost in velvet shroud,
Why in the night man fears to be alone
Beneath soft, silky quilts of wind and cloud.
This is my time and I have none to lose
Since the morning sun is certain to awake
The misty hours. Pen, paper now I choose
And I go out and find a path to take
To capture night upon the printed page
Before the sun obliterates the shade.
I search that night to sing for youth and sage.
I sing of that from which the night is made.

THE TWO HOUSES

The house I chose to build has many doors
From room to room and through the outer wall,
And I have rugs and carpets on the floors
To muffle noise time makes with each footfall.
I built with freedom to get out and in
Of this small house that stands a time in space,
To comfort me against thirst and the wind,
To have choice pets and flowers around my place.
I made this house with many windows too;
I could not have too many panes for light
In windows of my walls where I could view
Through their transparency the velvet night.
Someday, I'll have a house not of my choice
Without a pane betwixt me and the day,
No music, mirth, not one familiar voice
Or door or window in its walls of clay.

SACRED LAND OF YOUTHFUL DREAMS

When I last see farewell-to-summers bloom
Out in this autumn after killing frost,
I know that in my big Earth's lifetime room
I should journey here to count the cost.
Above me are blue skies and evening sun
That sends it splinters of a mellow light.
It was here that my high school themes were done,
This grove where pines are stricken now by blight.
How long, how far away when I came here
To write, and hanging lantern in a pine
I came when spring was green and autumn was
My favorite haunt on sacred land of mine.
I have returned to where writing began
After these fifty years of life have gone,
Returned to where I first became a man.
I have come here and I have come alone.
What is there to man's travail on this earth
With youthful dreams that haunted him since birth?

A WAY OF LIFE

To have this house surrounded by the wind,
This little unknown place wherein to live,
Nature to read and time like coins to spend,
To have a will to work and heart to give,
To help a neighbor in his time of need,
This is the way of life we know and keep;
Winter for leisure, spring for planting seed,
Summer for growth, autumn the time to reap.
We're like spring blades of tender April grass
That lift their heads toward the morning sun.
Like these our days are numbered and must pass
And our accomplishments are counted done.
When for one of us the link is broken
And by the laws of life he must depart,
Although we weep when our farewell is spoken,
We know he'll live forever in each heart

IT'S NOT THE WIND

It's not the wind in the weeping willow tree
Who speaks to me on a convalescing bed,
Placed by the window where I hear and see.
These are real voices, not dreams, in my head.
They have returned, these lovers long departed,
To this fair valley where they used to be.
They come unseen before spring blooms are shed
And talk and laugh and sing as merrily
As a pair of loving bluebirds in the spring
Who have a nest with eggs in our fence post.
Of all our birds the bluebirds love the most.
With April song they make this valley ring. . . .
They vie with lovers that I fail to see
Who talk and laugh beneath the willow tree.

STAY WHILE APRIL IS MY LOVER

Death, do not come for me when April's here.
I'm not the dead oak on the greening hill,
So lifeless, barren, pitiful, and still.
Select for me a death month of the year—
October or November, if you must.
Come after me but never come in April
When new life comes to me like chlorophyll
That rises up tree veins from earth's sweet dust.
Come in the red sun's cold-blue winter splendor.
Come January not to find me ready.
Just come to snoop around in February.
Come take my dust but leave my name and number.
I warn you, stay while April is my lover.
Her fleeting tenderness I must possess;
Her saturation point of creativeness,
Before I lie beneath an April cover.

TOSSING MINUTES TO THE SKY

Last night Time's crying winds in the sassafras
Were singing cool death songs for summer's ending.
These warning songs were truthful and befriending
When I arose to face the looking glass.
I saw the autumn in my face and hair
But I stood there unyielding and unbending
Without a comment on what Time was sending
By his cool calculating winds out there.
Through lips of sassafras Time's words were spoken.
I feared not these; nor would I be defending.
My autumn days I would too soon be spending.
Time's crying winds could never be a token
To warn me of the season when men die.
I'd keep on tossing minutes to the sky!

I'LL SING DESPITE IMMORTAL TIME

I'll sing of you despite immortal time,
You rugged hills that shoulder to the skies.
As free as blowing wind, I'll spin my rhyme
Of earth and time, love, joy, and wild night cries.
I'll sing of you—your everlasting rocks,
Brown monsters sprawling high in lazy sun.
I'll sing of coves, sweet tender blooming phlox.
I'll sing of hills until my day is done.
I'll sing my songs before it is too late
As no one else has ever sung before.
I'll sing sweet love, illicit love, and hate
And glorify old men in legend, lore.
I'll sing of headless men who have come back
On moonless nights to terrify their neighbors.
I'll sing of hill dance, moonshine, applejack,
And more than these before Time stops my labors.

DESCEND UPON US, NIGHT

Descend upon us, night of green spring love!
Descend upon us, O Great Night of Love!
The winds are wailing in the briary cove.
And we stand here alone, O Night of Love!
Those who have not felt eternal pulse of love
Know life is false and utter nothingness.
For them the muted winds upon the cove
Is lonesome wailing in the midnight darkness.
For us, the muted winds are violins
And life is strange and beautiful to own;
The violins of muted midnight winds,
The towering pine, the rugged mountain stone.
Descend upon us, Night of Love, for soon,
Too soon, the night of April love has flown.
Above green poplar leaves the same cold moon
Will ride above new lovers when we're gone.

GREAT NIGHT OF DARKNESS

Great Night of darkness holding me in void
Between your mountain of eternal dust,
Mine is the pen that Nature has employed.
Mine is the voice of song that she can trust.
Great Night, my living dust is still a part
Of mountain loam, of rock jut and clay.
And Earth's Creator put into my heart
A spark of fire to make me sing my lay!
I sing of lonesome waters and the shack
While there is strength of mountains in my blood.
I sing of love, dream, work, of corn and stack,
Of winter wind and April's flowery mood.
Great Night of darkness, when you have subdued
My body's strength and turned my eyes to stone,
Deafened my ears to sound and killed my mood,
I shall be dust to grow tough trees thereon.

LATE INTERVIEW

Yes, who am I to sit out in this autumn?
To see the multicolored leaves on trees
I knew as saplings on the slope and bottom
Where honeysuckle was up to my knees?
After the years wild birds still come to sing,
As they sang in this world when I was young.
Same species now that made my young world ring;
I thought their songs the sweetest ever sung.
I am enchanted by my late return
To see again old places of young dreams,
With multicolored autumn leaves that burn,
With little quietly flowing autumn streams.
Now in a place and time with my years few
To be a living man upon my earth;
Here I have come for this late interview,
Upon this autumn land that gave me birth.

WHEN AUTUMN INTERVENES

Leaves turn color only in the autumn.
They change from their spring-green and summer
    growth
To splashy, colored drops on hill and bottom,
Since wind blew early frost down from the North.
Frost cannot destroy leaf in autumn change
No more than autumn can destroy this man.
This flesh will live again in something strange;
Let autumn death do with it what it can.

There will be fears when autumn intervenes
Because this is the time when autumn must
Change greens to golds for coins for thriftless winds;
Rich autumn is season for the winds to trust.
But I hear moaning winds' eternal sounds,
Weeping for me, close to the leafstrewn ground.

OCTOBER LOVE

Your lips are red as mountain sourwood leaves
That hang upon the gray October bough;
Your voice is sweeter than the wind that grieves
Over this land alive with colors now.
Your pretty eyes have endless depths of blue
Like pools fringed by the bracken and the fern;
Your pretty face is autumn beech-leaf hue,
The fairest autumn color to discern.
What shall I do for you when autumn goes?
When sourwood leaves have fallen to the ground?
When cold snow-laden wind of winter blows
Through winter boughs unlike your sweet-voice
        sound?
I weep to think that autumn will be over
When winds have rained the beech leaves from the
        tree;
When mountain pools are under silent cover
And winter takes my autumn love from me.

SINCE I HAVE BEEN A BROTHER

Since I have been a brother to the dust
The years like lazy cattle have walked by.
The steel I polished once has turned to rust,
And days come back when I can hear the cry
Of long-drawn curses black as winter oaks,
From shouting pilots on the zooming cranes.
I still can hear air-hammers' mighty strokes
And feel the furnace heat in blistering pains.
But, Lord, is there a chance of turning back
The pages of my life at seventeen?
Those days are colorless as furnace slag. . . .
Ten hours each day, and lodgings were unclean.
The pencil marks of blood and steel and sweat
Are in my veins. . . . I know I can't forget.

BY THE BEND IN THE ROAD

You can't park here tonight: this is my nook.
The moon is up. I sit alone and wait
To hear frogs singing in this autumn brook,
To hear the cicadas now that summer's late.
Tobacco has been cut and strung on sticks,
Awaiting now high tierpoles in the barn.
The songs of frogs and cicadas don't mix
With songs from whippoorwills among the ferns.
I will sit here tonight while men make haste.
Where do they go? With whom? What are they after?
They desecrate the highway with their waste,
Unmindful to the songs of flowing water,
Unmindful of our world of night and moon,
So radiantly alive to die too soon!

EPITHALAMIUM AND EPITAPH

When I go forth let silence be my doom
And nothing solid mark where I am lain.
Because, I think, to share this little room
Beneath the windless patter of the rain
Is peace enough to close my tired eyes
To sunny vine-clad hills where crickets sing,
Blindly to sleep beneath the moonlit skies
And fern bouquets my mountain lovers bring.

It does not matter much when one is gone
Beneath a hillside world for quieter rest.
In spring the crows return; the world moves on
And storm winds rend the pinetops greener crest.
O, mountain lovers, stop where I am lain.
Stop and pluck roses for a nice bouquet.
Stop where the tall weeds spindle in the rain,
Weeds growing on my final room of clay.

I CANNOT WRITE TONIGHT

I cannot write tonight for the moon is full
And large as a wagon wheel above the timber.
I must go out, for the world is beautiful,
Must leave the open fire and dying ember.
For what are words upon an ink-stained scroll
When magic moonlight floods this stubborn world?
When wary winds of ruthless winter roll
Over the knolls, and leaves and sedge are hurled
Into illimitable starry space?
I must be out in beauty, hectic, rough,
On mountains big enough for my embrace.
I must be out where I can love enough. . . .
Remember, hills stay young; their beauty keeps
Eternally as seasons come and pass.
They will be here when this admirer sleeps,
Who will not leave his shadow on their grass.

MY LOVES WILL REMAIN WHEN I HAVE PASSED

My loves will remain when I have passed
Beyond this certainty of time and light
And positive decay. But surely this night
I shall remember. These spiral massed
Pine silhouettes against the horizon.
Nocturnal things have been my loves: moon-downs,
Valleys of fog and sleepy mountain towns,
Dew on the grass and play of wind upon
The hill. Night sounds I have loved: the cold
Nosing winds in November corn stubbles,
The zoom of wires and water that troubles
Creek mosses and ferns. Happier loves will unfold
When I have passed far beyond this night,
Beyond all loves and swimming time of light.

WHAT CAN THESE COLD WORDS DO?

What can these cold words do? Drop, drop, like rain.
Fall on the dead leaves, fall, drop, drop, drop, drop.
Fall on the winter grass. Again, again
Hear them ooze through the wind, drop, drop, drop,
    drop.
O I could cry up like a good night god
And tell eternity to leave my face
Blue under skin of earth upturned to sod;
My face blue-rot under the rain drenched sod.
What can these cold words matter when drip, drip,
Of rain comes down from barren winter trees
And winds whine over to strange destinies?
What can a poet do lost in these millions?
Lost in the dust for all oblivions?

TIME IS LATE

My sixty-seventh August, now diminished,
Is now recorded time, oblivion.
And, with its passing, my time is diminished.
Augusts are special months that pass too soon.
Transition from hot summer to cool autumn
With cidia singing sadly of their fate
In firefly light above our meadow bottom—
The cidia's singing warns me time is late.
Time now, most precious wealth I have to spend,
More than cash and collaterals I've amassed.
I need more time to serve me to the end,
Before all of my August months have passed.
Cool changing August months have all been excellent,
With sixty-seven each a paid receipt.
The Augusts of my life have been well spent;
Augusts to come, I will not know defeat.

The World
as Song
Singing Itself

A SINCERE SONG

Each morn I rise before my world awakes
And breathe sweet winds of morning from wild
    flowers;
I like soft sounds the early morning makes
While earth is snoring in her twilight hours.
I like the sincere songs of rising birds
Who put new life into beginning day;
Birds' songs are better than a poet's words
In mild midsummer's early roundelay.
Softly I walk upon my waking world
Where little lyric streamlets speak to me;
Where brown-eyed susans' petals are dew-curled,
Their dark eyes winking at eternity.
A few midsummers more the birds will miss
My searching when the morning winds have died;
Ghost-figure in the quietness of mists,
Searching for something, never satisfied.

GREEN RIVER

Green winter river flowing to the sea
Between snow-covered banks and barren trees,
I speak to you and you speak back to me
With interruptions of a winter breeze.
In seasons past my love and I have stood
Beneath your willow, elm, and sycamore,
And hummed tunes to the music of your flood,
And written lyrics to your lilting roar.
We do not always sing and make a rhyme
In spring beneath your fluffy, green-cloud shade;
We go to you in leaf and blossom time
And in these hours with you our dreams are made.
Flow on; take to warm seas your winter ice
Down rippling green between white strips of foam.
But bring spring back, days balmy, warm, and nice;
We'll make your winding course our springtime home.

JOYOUSLY TO DRIFT AND DREAM

Beneath green clouds I do not walk alone
Into the quietness of solitude.
I have for company a tree, flower, and stone,
A singing stream and blowing wind for mood.
I make my bed beside the gnarled braceroots
Of stalwart beech, upon the leaf-strewn ground;
Beside the mandrake and sweet anise shoots;
This convalescing bed is best I've found.
I lie, my back on dead leaves, looking through
Green leaves into the windy-blue of May
While crows fly down to have an interview
Alighting on boughs fifty feet away.
Consoling are the tunes of futile wind.
Soft are the lullabies from singing stream.
So soothingly they penetrate my mind
And send me joyously to drift and dream.

SPIRIT GROWTH

Lie down and feel winds crawling over me.
Look up to see the mares' tails brushing sky.
And all about me strange eternity
While on the grass beneath a tree I lie.
As I look up from here life is serene,
Patterned by a symphony of wind;
Best place in life's expansion I have been
For I have learned men must grow from within.
Mind can expand by giving time its own.
Can heart control the mind or mind the heart?
Let them decide out in this world alone
Or work in unison, each do its part.
Body relaxed upon this quilt of grass—
It could lie here in spirit growth forever,
To live in wind, to watch a white cloud pass.
I will not reach such height again—no, never!

SHINGLEMILL SYMPHONY

I have escaped the little schools of thought,
Some single theory of some righteous way,
In Shinglemill's cool valley where peace brought
A symphony that nature's poets play.

Unwarped creative minds won't subjugate
My stirring moods that cry aloud for birth.
I'm here with them; they leave me to my fate:
A restless rebel contemplating worth.

No one can dictate dreams for me to write.
Alone here I can be original,
Explore dark corners of creative night
Where moonlight's lengthening blue shadows fall.

Night is around me now. Why am I here?
Do I hear wings above me in the wind?
In valley lonesome as a funeral bier,
I search for destiny and find a friend.

To walk a cattle path up Shinglemill
That parallels a winding, dwindling stream.
On either side there is a rugged hill;
To walk this valley is to dream a dream.

The white-faced cattle find the waterhole.
The hummingbird drinks nectar from the phlox.
The bluebird flies into her nesting bole.
A lizard suns upon a lichen rock.

Sing "Nellie was a lady," soft and slow.
Sing like the vibrant splinters from the spheres.
"When I was seeing Nellie home" .ˑ. . Sing low;
Renew the cadences of passing years.

I walk into this dream for peace is here
That comes with cidias' soft evening song;
They tell me summer's gone and autumn's near
And Shinglemill's the place where I belong.

The restful seizure in this autumn wood,
Grasshopper, cidia, and katydid,
Pour forth their music in a cloudburst flood.
If voice was steam they'd lift the kettle lid.

I lie in sourwoodshade in semi-sleep
While years behind me roll beyond my sight.
The valley called eternity is deep;
I look below into its endless night.

So careful not to walk too close the brink,
Through restful seizure I have entered dream.
And now it does not matter what I think
When I awake beside the dwindling stream.

Where pawpaw trees hang heavy with ripe fruit
And music makers still are piping loud,
I know that blossoms better are than loot
As I look through green leaves at a white cloud.

For I must stay where my heart is at ease;
I've lost my larger world now part by part.
And to my valiant heart I must say "please,"
And from my larger world I must depart.

My smaller world was once a single room,
A table, chair, and bed on which I slept.
When this could not expand I lived in gloom;
I lay in darkness on my bed and wept.

My cell grew to a house and then a yard
Where I had sun and shadow in my grasp.
And with the blades of grass much time I shared;
I had time for the butterfly and wasp.

My house and yard were worlds I'd never known,
Because I'd no time left to mop my brow.
Good life I once lamented, that had flown;
My new world boundaries were growing now.

I pushed the narrow bound'ries of my world
That gave both ease and comfort to my heart.
With strength regained, my challenges unfurled;
The circle that enclosed me fell apart.

I welcomed once anew old life I loved,
The world I roamed on land, on seas, through skies.
My heart beat valiant for me while I roved;
Each day I lived as fast as life's time flies.

And I returned to table, bed, and chair,
Away from jets that fly as fast as sound,
Away from food and smoke that I held dear.
I came back to the April grass and found

Each little blade a stirring universe,
Each butterfly and wasp my friend again.
My heart at ease directed my life's course;
A new world for the one I'd sought to gain.

Autumn is late love rich in monotone,
Last little time left for our love's last fling.
Remember, dear, our yesterdays have flown.
How sure are we about the second spring?

We are the cool selected living dust
With eyes to see the beauty in each other;
Our lips have met so often, for they must
In our attractiveness for one another.

How rich in monotone is autumn's singing
Where cidias speak of love on every tree;
And rooster redbird's vibrant voice is ringing
For her from birth to her eternity.

And I am singing on my written page
For all who will lend me an ear to listen;
At fifty-eight I'm not inactive sage,
For in me autumn sparks of love still glisten.

What am I doing here? And who am I?
Don't ask me for I'm sure I've never known.
I know I'm man: my thoughts race to the sky
And joyfully I've loved each year that's flown.

Since I came to this world love's normal cause,
You had as well ask me about a star.
Billions have lived and died by natural laws.
No, you had better question who you are,

And search for truth and tell me what you find.
Living together in this world in love,
Exchanging highest thoughts from heart and mind,
In our brief journey here we should approve.

First: know thyself and to thyself be true
And fill with love each emptiness within.
Then you will know what I have tried to do,
Beneath the sky upon my path of wind.

Here in these deep dark woods is mystery.
Here in this formlessness love lies concealed.
This beech, initial-scarred, now holds the key.
Here's evidence on a back-to-nature field.

Here is a spring beneath a sycamore
With snake-coiled roots to siphon water in.
Here ragweeds carpet a primeval floor
And there are whispers from the lazy wind.

Love has been here to leave its little mark
Of those who sat beneath this tall beech shade.
They left initials on its hard-green bark
While they were young before their dreams were
        made.

To what far ends of earth have lovers gone
From this wild place, deep in this wilderness?
Do any of these sleep without a stone?
Are these the last marks of their happiness?

Amid a million trees born on this slope
With interlocking roots that savor soil,
Many are born without a ray of hope.
Death spares them from their endless growing toil.

To succor nourishment for every tree
Will feed majority and famish few.
In dead young trees there is no mystery
When winter dies and spring revives anew.

The carcass of a wooden hulk will fall
To nourish roots of those that caused its death.
Among surviving trees birds stop to call;
They sing a note of cheer and waste their breath.

Amid our humankind our stalwart perish
Of burdens, in our free society.
They succor sustenance for those to nourish
Who won't accept responsibility.

Life is much better out where leaves are dying,
Where there is music in the dry wind's crying,
And where birds gather for their southbound flying.
Life is much better lying on the ground.

Life is much better where wild ferns are nodding,
And where the thirsty terrapin is plodding
Toward the dwindling stream for watering.
Over dead leaves he makes a ticklish sound.

Phlegmatic copperhead, imbued with hating,
Has felt the time has come for hibernating.
Instinctively his mind is contemplating
Where hibernation places can be found.

Out here upon the ground, where I am lying,
All of the autumn months will soon be spying
On every creature crawling, walking, flying.
Somewhere in Shinglemill I'll be around.

O WHAT A POEM I AM IN

The whole earth around me now is in rhythm. It is an autumn poem with rhythmic measure. Autumn, fast winds, slow winds, and no winds accent this physical poetic masterpiece! Try walking in and on and over a poem like this autumn one just one time! Hear it chanted! Get full of it, as I am now, and see if you can describe how you feel! You just try putting autumn's poetic rhythms into words!

There is a special rhythm to the wing-beats of wild birds on the wind—slicing the October wind, which I believe has color! People say the wind doesn't have color but this wind, which is a part of this poem, rhythm and wing-beat, I think is the color of white wine. Maybe it isn't, but it looks this way today.

And I feel and know rhythm in this autumn earth poem as I walk under trees—a forest of giant and small trees—many species of trees—and now with many colors of leaves. And I know the earth around—now in a maze of colors—is in rhythm. I know it is! And there are beats and light beats—soft beats and little hard beats as I look up to the tops of trees—out through multicolored peepholes to the sky. And the leaves come down with rhythmic rustles of the wind, which is like white wine—I breathe deep and don't drink it. Leaves, leaves, leaves come down and hit my face.

Sway trees—ride on the wind, leaves! Tree branches, play! Claw with your fingertips—your leafy fingertips—sough with your green-bark lips—rhythm through the feathery leaves—rhythm through the green pine needles—rhythmic wind that soughs, sings, and wheedles—now through—sough through—wheedle through—needle through winds and leaves and trees. I'm memorizing you. What a poem you are! Fit to be read to sun and moon and star! A poem that won't be read but will be from memory said! Down, leaves, and hit my face! Fly leaves just anyplace. Ride on the wind that's blowing out and blowing in. Leaves, leaves, so many colored birds—riding on the winds over this autumn earth—so many birds, so many periods for my written words—periods to hold poetic lines on this poetic autumn earth.

I'm out of the woods and leaves and to this place —where only white wine wind can hit my face! Here are the slopes of sterile earth—covered with sedge —good old brown broomsedge—a cover for the rabbit, grouse, and quail. And all this sedge is now a-quiver—in autumn rhythm that cannot go on forever. Trees in motion, falling leaves—winds that laugh and winds that grieve—winds that make the sedgegrass quiver—autumn winds, yes, autumn winds that can't go on forever. Don't be frightened, rabbit, quail, and grouse—you've just got the wind a-coming in your house—playing with sedge that you hide in —playing with sedge enough to make it quiver! All earth is rhythmic now but this can't be forever! Winds will get tired and want some rest. They will lie down upon the leaves they have blown to the ground. It will be best for earth, trees, leaves, when winds lie down to get some rest.

Some putting sounds of dots and dashes—the silver maple leaves now trembling in the sun—white dots —white dashes on the winds make splashes. Sure, these carry messages that chipmunks and mice will read. Sounds on the wireless birds and wildlife will heed.

I see the silver wires up there—electric—telephone—up trembling in the sun—must be large silver gossamer wires giant spiders have spun. I look for spiders but they are not up there and not coming down the air—with anchored strands they are unraveling everywhere.

Oh, what a poem I am in! Over my head—under my feet—and on each side of me—up level with my eyes. Here is that rhythmical earth poem which is man-size—a poem for eternity. Sway through, play through—slow through—blow through poetic leaves for me to catch hold! Come over multicolored leaves and dash and splash my face. Give me poetic messages you are sending out where tree branches and the sedge are bending.

Looking at my Sandy River like a sea! The winds have blown small waves of destiny! Can you believe that winds can wrinkle water—wrinkle-soft surface of the Sandy River—to make the crane and shikepoke shake with laughter?

Can you believe the winds have placed upon my

Sandy River leaf galleons and multicolored ships to sail forever? No, they won't sail forever—where rhythmic waters tremble—old leaf ships will overturn and sink and winds will bring new ones to reassemble.

Laugh on, you long-billed crane! Stand propped upon a Sandy River floating log! As long as you stand there you'll leave the little fish alone. Feathery up on silken climbing wings—slow flying, up and up into the autumn rhythm until you are a part! And little homely shikepoke takes over where you stood—your leaving didn't break a heart!

> Along my Sandy River
> The reeds and waterlilies quiver.
> The golden eyes of daisies plead.
> Soil, water, sun are all they need
> To spread a white and golden sheet
> Over a bottom for the tall cranes' feet,
> A lush green carpet for the tall cranes' feet.

Away from water—away from Sandy River to my woods where tough-butted white oaks long have stood—tough trees that gather little sustenance from the clay—a stubborn tree that likes to have its way. A tree from childhood all mixed up. Sometimes I think old tough-butt thinks it is a buttercup. But legend has it that this tree—growing in our hardwood tree country—wanted to be an evergreen—but old Mother Nature intervened. And this is why I have come here to see my white oak trees. And true to form they will not shed their leaves—winds blow through —slow through—their finger twigs—as tough as wires—as sharp as briars they hold their leaves.

If winds prefer—just let them grieve—poem of rhythmic earth—these white oaks are some chosen part. A lyric in this earth's big poem—to memorize with mind and say with heart. These hardwoods trying to be evergreens. Well, in the spring the new buds push away the winter leaves. And spring wind laughs but never grieves.

Today I am as high as wind is high! I am a part of autumn's rhythmic rhyme—a part of this, the greatest poem of our time. I will stay out here until the winds lie down to rest. And rest for them will be the best. I will be here a part as falls the leaf—a dot—a dash upon my face with a message beautiful and brief. This stops the rhythm of my magic earth, which is a part of me and I a part of it—this poem since my birth!

MORNING INTERVIEW

Too early for the hungry birds to stir,
Yet I arise and go out in the cold
To look up through the winding, windy stair
At a million stars of brilliant, shiny gold.
I hear the stream's soft whispers under ice
As worried winter winds start to rehearse
An inconsistent song that can't suffice,
To top wind songs of this small universe.
Under eternal roof of gold and blue
With earth's uncertain carpet at my feet,
I'm happy with this morning interview
That lifts me from the clutches of defeat.
After a walk in my front yard I find,
Inspiration, like lightning, strikes my mind.

DREAM HARVEST

I'm lonely as this autumn night for you
While you accept the comforts of the bed
To slumber while I walk the long night through
With moods enough to stir the sleeping dead.
These barren trees with tangled berry vines
Are obstacles that try to fence me in.
My heart says I must drink the night-mood wines
And like a lovesick fox run wild with wind.
Poetic moods will never let me sleep
On my soft bed with a clean sheet for my cover;
Not when love's dream is young to catch and keep,
When sleep to come will be my long-last lover.
In my dream harvest I walk on imploring,
While you lie in your calm oblivious slumber.
Dawn's light will find me lonely in the morning.
Not night and walking, but you I'll remember!

RAILROAD SOUNDS

I have heard mean groans of heavy engines
Striking the emptiness of night.
And I have heard the drive wheels slipping
At Black Mountain when the track was sanded.
Those sounds I have heard and loved.

I have heard the lonesome whistle screaming
When a bright light was leading,
A red light trailing,
And the naked train moaned with the wind.

I have heard the oozing steam from slick pistons,
The swinging and banging of box car doors.
And I have heard the winter winds
Whip the frozen wiring
And tear across the bitter sky.
These sounds I have loved.

LOVESONG FOR APRIL

You know I can no longer sit with ease
In my soft chair before this cheerful flame,
When April is out there among the trees
Dancing on a path the bright moon came.
Dearest, on other nights your winsomeness,
Your clever words, your soft caressing hand,
Kisses from lips of magic you possess
Held me obedient to your command.
No longer can you hold me prisoner,
Subdue me with the magic of your kiss,
When April's calling me to be with her,
To share her love upon a night like this.
I shall kiss her soft wind-lips tenderly
When we embrace in ambient ecstasy.

THE FLOWER GATHERER

I shall go out today and gather flowers
Or leave them if I choose still on the stem.
I shall go out and fool away the hours
Beside the murmuring Little Sandy stream.
And I shall go beside that stream today
To find a bouquet for Naomi Deane
Before the wind blows all the blooms away.
I'll gather phlox and mix primrose between.
This is the time to put all work behind
Since it is season of the bloom and bud;
When blossoms swell their fragrance to the wind,
And earth and man are in a joyful mood.
Love in my heart and brain is revived now.
I haven't time to walk behind my plow.

I LOVE NOT SPRINGTIME LESS

I love not springtime less but summer more:
The smell of growing corn, the silken mats
Of sawbriar hair, wind-combed; the damp earth floor
Of tousled weeds, of brush, and poplar flats.
I love the harvest moon, the drifting skies.
I love the wild rose petals on the hills
And July wheat stacks filled with wild birds' cries;
Life-ever-lasting, drying snail thin-shells.
I love oak bark, the lizard's tight-lipped mouth;
The red sweet-williams growing on a bank,
The little streams of swallows going south,
And horseweeds by the river growing rank.
I love blue glimmer of the cornfield haze,
And such slow passing of the summer days.

APRIL IS LIFE

Here on my porch I watch new daffodils
To see their golden blooms burst from green rind,
To see each blossom feeling of the wind;
Life won't allow me many more young Aprils.
Another cloud comes over with a shower
To green the woodland moss into a cover,
To put spring life into sweet meadow clover,
To put first blossoms on the wildwood flower.
The redbird flies to an oak upon the hill;
The ground squirrel darts into his hole.
The bluebird sticks her head out from a hole;
A crow flies over with straws in his bill.
April is life and wind is Spring's sweet breath.
How many thousand years have come and gone?
How many thousand more will linger on
To resurrect new life in the face of death?

TO BE JUST ONE OF THEM

Invisible slice of time coloring green,
Moodsong for valley and for rock-capped hill—
This annual resurrection we call April
Is born today amid a winter scene.
Ten million fluffy flakes spiraling down
To cover brown leaf carpet under timber
Is magic April's birth, crows will remember,
With each pine weighted in a snowy gown.
April is born beneath a blinded moon,
This month, for great rejoicing and rebirth,
When winter sleepers will rise up from earth
And the worm turns butterfly in its cocoon.
Beginning now, beneath the world's wide rim
The earth will soon be seething at its seams
To resurrect ten billion living dreams!
I will go out and be just one of them.

PROLIFIC DIRT

By-product of prolific dirt am I;
Alive, ambitious, walk and talk and sing.
My mind can travel depths from earth to sky;
In winter I can see and write of spring.
The substance of prolific dirt is tree;
Adjustable to climate and to clime.
This dirt can die, can live, has destiny,
Is nondestructible to passing time.
Prolific dirt is substance of the flower,
Its stem, bud, blossom, lead, and silken petal,
A loveliness that haunts us in its hour;
Prolific dirt, our dream, our fight, our metal!
Basis for beauty, life, and all desire,
Retainer of the millions gone before,
Bulwark against the bomb, immune to fire,
Prolific dirt, eternal evermore!

I WOULD LOVE FREEDOM

I would love freedom such as I once knew
When spring returned to hills, to coves and hollows,
With April sun to drink the morning dew,
And bright-winged butterflies above the meadows.
I would love airy April's spacious room
With wind washed fluffy-clean by thunder showers,
Scented by bush in multicolored bloom,
By sawbriar tendril, phlox, and percoon flowers.
I would love freedom of the gold-winged bee
But not of minnows little creeks confine,
That I may walk forever just to see
Again this brain-embedded world of mine.
My heart and brain keep flying to this earth
That holds my past, my present, and my future,
Whose April beauty fed this brain from birth
And whose loam gave this body growth and nurture.

MAN AND HIS VALLEY

Valley with lyric voice in winter wind,
What lies beyond your depths of stirring sound?
Trees are etched on soft evening's blue blind.
Old restive leaves are wood nymphs on the ground.
I am man's living symbol of your clay
And cool dirt words you speak are not in vain.
I thirst for you when I have gone away.
Tonight I drink,
     But I shall thirst again.
My valley of the close eternal tie,
When you are gay,
     I am filled with delight.
And when you grieve and autumn night winds cry,
I walk enthralled into your starry night.
What lies hidden?
     I do not understand
Infinite wisdom of this workable plan,
That everything is oneness with the land
When you are valley, and I am the land.

ACTIVE SUMMER MOVES TOO FAST

Swallows are flying over crabgrass meadows;
Through high bright sheets of wind they wheel and
    dart.
Trailed on the sun-drenched land by flirting shadows,
They're gathering contentment on my heart.
I hear their preening wings slice winds in August
That sigh through nooks the killdees have forgotten.
I see a broken pinion on the dust;
The ants work on this pinion old and rotten.
I know this active summer moves too fast,
And as leaves turn, summer more swiftly goes.
Minutes are in the first leaves blowing past;
Minutes are going with the wind that blows.
Summer is ending when the swallows gather
And practice flying South in any weather.

FRESH BREATHS OF LIFE

Walk out into invigorating cool
At six when our October world awakes,
When our surrounding world is beautiful.
Magnificent this world where each partakes
Of breathing cool, clean, unpolluted air.
Feel winy mountain air seep through your clothes;
Feel it deep in your lungs and on your skin;
Sensations man today so seldom knows,
Mornings when he walks in October wind.
After the years have bent his stalwart frame
Cold breaths of air that he is walking through,
This man, the world will never know his name,
Attached to time and place in his review
Of his small world where days have been the same
Day after day and in his yesteryears.
Now he walks out to take fresh breaths of life,
In time his last before the final fears
Ending Octobers and his mortal strife.

NO TIME TO LOSE

April in my Kentucky is for me,
Where my plows turn the mellow April sod,
Where blossoms cluster on the wild plum tree,
Where milkweed furze is growing in the pod.
There is no breathing equal to the sniff
Of fresh-turned loam, roots severed from the tree.
I put my face against the furrow: if
Fresh loam root-scented can't put in me
Fresh vigor with strength of stalwart hill
I will walk shoulder-high in April texture.
There I shall find the aromatic wind that will
When I breathe deeply standing like a fixture.
Earth-scented wind, soft dirt words from my plow,
Wild birds now flying over ones and twos,
Dogwoods and redbuds wreathe each hilly brow.
Kentucky April, I've no time to lose.

THE HEART FLIES HOME

Though you are there tonight and I am here
You must not doubt my heart does not fly home
To you, when autumn leaves are brown and sere
And stars are bright as honey in the comb.
Designs of leaves are in the dress you wear,
As you walk where the autumn leaves jump down
From tall treetops into your autumn hair.
There sere leaves fall until earth wears a gown.
After a walk you sit before the fire
Feeling the cheerful heat from oak and pine,
Reading a book till midnight, then retire
To a clean, cool bed in a home that's yours and mine.
If wheels will roll on rails of shining steel
And wings will climb up mountains of bright wind,
Soon I shall be with you where we can feel
The time is now and leave the past behind.

WHEN THERE IS MUSIC

Thank God I have a Love who goes with me
When there is music in the wind at night;
On mountains where boughs weave incessantly
Between us and the moon and pale starlight.
Immortal symphonies are played by wind
Of destiny that sweeps the upland cone.
Night wind in pines is a crying violin;
Night wind in oaks is a tenor saxaphone.
Night wind in sassafras is a magic flute;
Through sourwood branches a soft-toned guitar.
In sawbriar tendrils night wind is a lute,
Beneath the floating cloud, the moon and star.
We store a portion of this symphony
To live unwritten in our heart and brain;
We live a night of love and poetry,
A night of nights we hope will come again.

NIGHT WIND'S SERENADE

In the music of this night wind's serenade
I heard the snowbirds reach high plaintive notes;
And April's meadowlarks in orchard shade
Pipe on a dozen silver-throated flutes.

I hear outside a hundred violins
And swelling magic from pipe organ keys;
Until this house is shaken by the winds
That soon subside to sounds of rustling leaves.

But I arise from bed to pull the shade,
To let a strip of winter moonlight in;
I cannot sleep when a symphony is played
By instruments in an orchestra of wind.

How can I sleep when night is bright as day?
When winter moonlight floods this hungry land?
I look out where the young musicians play;
I see no motions of a director's hand.

Out there I now hear falling of soft rain,
Tapping bright, autumn earth's new gold-leaf cover;
I hear the voice of youth on a dusty lane
And know the best for them is not yet over.

I hear the music that the years have known,
Of mountain rivers gliding to the sea;
Over the sand shoals and the cool slate stone,
Waters that flow and sing perpetually.

I hear bells at the close of autumn day
Above the rustling blades of ripening corn;
I hear bright leaves and winds of morning play
And the far-off piping of a hunter's horn.

The world is in this symphony's refrain,
And I lie down again and close my eyes;
Hoping that it will bear me home again,
Beyond bleak hills where April's rivers rise.

SEND ME A MEMENTO

Why send me this old book that bores?
Dry bones that rustle in a corpse?
Send me a summer wind from home;
Just any kind of wind will do.
Send me a last leaf of the summer;
Just any kind of leaf will do:
Pawpaw, sourwood, or sassafras,
Memento of a season's passing,
A season never to return again.
I will return your book that bores,
But send me wind and send me leaf
Of a season that has been too brief.

TO BE A POET

My voice is not strong,
but won't you listen?
I tell you again and again
  I have something to say.
I have walked
  in the silence
    of the night.
I have talked
  to the stars.
I have tried
  to be strong
    as the oak trees
      I have leaned against
    and on whose bark
      I have put my hands.

I NEVER TRIED TO WRITE A BOOK

No, Sir, I never tried to write a book.
My pencil traced the sounds of high winds blowing
And sketched a willow-aggravated brook
And made some pictures of the green grass growing.
Word-drew a peddler in a thread-bare suit.
World-drew a new moon piece of cleared ground.
It pictured oak-brown leaves and red plum fruit,
White windy skies and water's lonely sound.
The hand that touched the pencil and the brain
That told the hand to shove the pencil on
Did not write this for profit, loss, and gain.
They wrote before my body's food was gone,
For words are slow to buy a poet bread.
Sometimes his words will sell when he is dead.

SPRING AND THE LARK

I lay in bed this morning while the lark
Burst out in song like blossoms in the spring;
The eastern light was pushing through the dark
And earth reborn inspired this lark to sing.
The branches of the elm it sat among
Were newly leafed and swished my window pane;
I lay as still as death to hear its song
And the distant answer of a lark's refrain.
I saw it rise and heard its spreading note
Of soft bird-music on the purpling light;
Music to wake spring earth from its small throat
After the silence of the long dark night.
Then I arose from bed and wept because
I could not stir my lover with a song,
For she would find it full of little flaws
And only spring to sing and it's not long.

SONG FOR ETERNAL SPRING

No one has sung for us, and may I sing
As one of us, for all of us, my songs,
Though futile as the mountain winds that fling
Their fluffy silver bellies on these throngs
Of jutted hills oak-crowned against the skies?
I sing of mountain men, their lives and loves,
And mountain waters and the wild bird cries,
And percoon blooming in the late March coves.
It's fun to run on iron legs and shout
Songs to the wind my blood has left unsung;
The tunes at home they never thought about,
Too busy living life while they were young.
I'll keep on singing long as this blood flows
And brain keeps active in this living head.
I'd like eternal spring when this blood goes
To sing among friends of the mountain dead.

BOY'S WORLD

When I was a boy the moon was brass;
The sun was a golden eye.
My April valley fenced by hills
Was roofed with violet sky.

When I was a boy my nickel bought
All the candy I could eat,
And there was a path to the country store
I ran on swift bare feet.

And there was a stream I used to wade
Where silver minnows swam;
When I looked in I saw a boy
Who was thc man I am.

When I was a boy I had my world
Wherein to grow and dream;
With chores to do to make me strong
So I could swim upstream.

I would not trade that world I knew
For the man's world I am in;
I'd like to be that barefoot boy
Running in the wind!

MY SUMMER VALLEY

I walk down my summer valley
To see the morning sun come up,
While fluid winds are fresh with scent
From meadow grasses to my knees.

My summer valley speaks to me
While birds are flying to their nests,
Worms in their bills to feed their young.
Grasshoppers sing on green cornstalks.

The noisy stream where water chokes
And gurgles over stones and sands
Has sunlit pools where minnows dart
To breakfast on the fallen insects—

A cricket, worm, grasshopper, bug.
The bright eye of the sun looks down
Onto my summer valley where
White mists rise up to meet blue skies.

My summer valley is a world
Within my reach, and I can fold
It round me like a cloak to wear
All over earth, where people say:
"Here is a man we love and trust."

PERFECTION NOW

Who was or is earth's greatest architect?
I've searched through all our fifty states at home.
I have found beauty great but not perfect,
And I have lived in Egypt, Greece, and Rome,
Where ancients sought the greatest and the best.
Now much in ruins, earth's people go to see
Beauty through centuries that stood the test.
Creators' names will last eternally.
While lying here beneath this leafy beech,
I cannot see through branches to the sky.
This architecture is beyond man's reach,
And seeing this has made me wonder why
Man can't excel the symmetry of trees,
Shape leaves and place them rightly on the bough.
Great Nature is the architect of these.
Billions of years of growth, perfection now!

*The World
as Springtime
Kentucky Hills*

O FLOWERY SPRINGTIME WORLD

O flowery springtime world in lilting blossom,
O flowery world of martin and the bee,
O world, if I could clutch you to my bosom,
You are such lover for these eyes to see!
All day I've walked in lonely white-top meadows;
All day I've watched birds carrying sticks and straws;
I've watched the slender poplars' quivering shadows
And crows by twos and heard their love caw-caws.
O flowery spring with sky and bird and tree,
Terrapin, turtle, and the ladybug,
With hornet, wasp, and golden honeybee,
And pairs of snakes upon earth's velvet rug.
O flowery spring and each mate to his love,
The water blue, the wind of April cool,
White sails of clouds on wind-blown ships
    above . . .
O flowery springtime world so beautiful!

MILKWEEDS AND SCOTTISH THISTLE

The milkweeds and the purple Scottish thistle
Flaunt to the wind their summer-scented blooms.
And by their stems the petaled silkweeds nestle
And flaunt to summer winds a sweeter bloom.
We roam the pasture fields when not at plowing
And pin the silkweed blossoms to our bosom,
And fling the milkweed furze to some wind blowing.
We pluck the sweet wild purple thistle blossom.
We love the smell of heated pasture grass.
We love the sun that wilts the shoestring vines.
We love the summer dome of high blue glass
Where sun rays drip the color of old wine.
We love the summer written in the grass,
This growing season that is slow to pass.

THEIR EYES HAVE SEEN

He sees them walking slowly by the stream,
Their small hands holding book and dinner pail.
They are awake to life and do not dream;
They shout to wind and mock the calling quail
With laughter ringing through the thin blue air,
As boys run for the old persimmon grove
To pick up mellowed fruit frost-ripened there,
To share with little rose-lipped girls they love.
This wakes the old man's dreams and memories
Of life that goes back fifty years and more
When coming home from school he pillaged these
Wild groves for the lady by him in the door,
Whose hair, like his, is white as moonlit snow.
Each morn and afternoon they watch them pass,
Remembering youth carefree as winds that blow
And steps once light as raindrops on the grass.

TOO SOON, TOO EARLY

Virginia flycatchers above my door
Though purring winter penetrates each breeze;
There's snow on hands and fingers of the trees
And a soft white carpet on earth's somber floor.
Too early in the time of blinded moon,
Cool for groundhog to leave his earthen bed,
When old love dreams stir in his sleepy head,
And butterfly won't break from her cocoon,
Woven by parent worm around a briar.
How can she speak with pride of ancestry,
Of famous bloodlines, proper pedigree,
When she is beauty queen on April air?
Too early still for earth's strong April heart
To send her waking tremors through the land,
While winter sends his drifts of snow-white sand;
Too soon for April's avalanche to start.

SPIRIT OF DAUNTLESS MEN

Springtime has come to them that do not know
Springtime is here, and yellow moon is under
A summer bank of clouds white as the snow.
Springtime is here with rain and heavy thunder.
Sprit of dauntless men, come back to us
And with your spirit help us make the new.
Cannot you dream that something lacks in us
To execute a whole and drive it through?
Somehow we wander deep within the night,
Unmindful now of you in grass and bloom.
Like smothered stems of grass we strive for light
And somehow fear to meet no certain doom.
Do our veins have your bloods? Our legs your bones?
Are we as solid as our mountain stones?

APRIL'S CALL

Young winds of April pass this jailhouse by
Where men lie on their prison cots and swear.
They hear young April answer with a sigh,
Spring month most beautiful with bluest air.
Winds tell them of the paths old foxes take
And channels where the bright clean waters run;
Of pretty dark-loam furrows plowboys make.
Winds tell them of May apples in the sun.
Winds whisper of their hills where they belong,
Where there is freedom of the earth and skies;
Where they could hear their wind and water's song
And have their elbow room for exercise.
Now they are shut away from all of this.
Between them and these winds are walls and bars.
They must lie here and dream of all they miss,
Sunshine and homes and hounds beneath the stars.

ENCHANTED APRIL

Enchanted April we shall see no more
Remained with us awhile but left too soon;
After she covered scars on earth's dark floor
With carpets for our eyes and sun and moon.
And where have bright young winds of April gone,
Who left their songs embedded in each heart?
Where are wild irises on gray sandstone?
Why do they and their blossoms now depart?
The rain-washed petals on the dogwood trees,
Starched by the night, pressed by the morning sun,
Have fallen like rain through eternities
Until each white bough is a barren one.
Why should one grieve to see this April pass
When it leaves history on futile grass?

RESURRECTION REASONING

Into an April wood when early green
Splashes the somber slopes of sleeping hills,
Where there have come and gone so many Aprils
And lonely life is lifted with this scene
Of magic resurrection from the earth,
Sentinel oaks without a leaf or bud
In senseless wind dream nothingness: sap-blood
Will soon give these tall giants a new rebirth.
No stranger in these woods when April comes
To resurrect life for another season;
Questions my heart has asked, my mind must reason
Amid the wild birds' songs and bee-loud hums.
The gray-green lichen on the cold sandstone
Is waiting for the lizards to crawl over.
Bees will be buzzing on the blooming clover
When resurrection reasoning is done.

THIS SIDE OF ETERNITY

Sunset has turned the Sandy to bright gold
From hill to hill where troubled waters roll.
Beauty of wealth is too much to behold;
Only high walls and valley can control.
We've never seen another scene like this:
Light, golden sunball in a flaming sky,
Late afternoon, minutes of fleeting bliss
Where winds above the golden waters cry
For scenic wonder that will soon be gone.
High on the oval hills the trees' dark stems
And long enduring ledges of cliffstone
Betwixt us and the sun have turned to gems.
Our flooded Sandy yellowed with farm clay
The sun transforms to gold for us to see.
For miracles we do not go away;
They are on this side of eternity.

THE DREAM THAT ONLY LOVE CAN MAKE

I hear harpbeats of crows' wings on the air
Under a smokeless arc of April skies;
Love pair on a bright wind avenue up there
Who see love sparkle in each other's eyes.
Their sweet caw-caws break silence on my farm
Above my meadows and my greening wheat.
Heads thrust to wind, their wings are arm to arm.
They stroll the avenue to their retreat,
Top branches of a pine high on the hill.
They anchored well their nest to this tall pine;
Wise, ancient birds, they built it with a will,
Built with their medieval design.
While she sits in nest silk on folded legs
He stands staunch guard against both hawk and snake,
And carries food and drink until the eggs
Bring forth the dream that only love can make.

EYE OF THE APRIL SUN

The eye of April's sun is a lovely thing,
A wagon wheel up there too bright to look at.
In the corner of its eye it holds the spring.
It holds growth, mysteries, and such as that!
Has arms of gold and fingers golden splints,
This shining eye we never take for granted;
Comptroller of a thousand household hints
That can draw water when its rays are slanted;
Can hurry lizards from long hibernation
To sun-warmed spots on lichen'd log or stone.
Sun-love begets new lizard population
In ecstasy before young April's flown.
Tra-la, tra-la, tra-la, eye of the sun,
Our loving friend to brighten April here,
Now is the time to get our planting done;
Another April and another year!

HOLD APRIL

Hold on to April; never let her pass!
Another year before she comes again
To bring us wind as clean as polished glass
And apple blossoms in soft, silver rain.
Hold April when there's music in the air,
When life is resurrected like a dream,
When wild birds sing up flights of windy stair
And bees love alder blossoms by the stream.
Hold April's face close yours and look afar;
Hold April in your arms in dear romance.
While holding her look to the sun and star
And with her in her faerie dreamland dance.
Do not let April go but hold her tight,
Month of eternal beauty and delight.

WORLD OF SPRINGTIMES PAST

Like moth wings in warm spring her dreams instead
Stir where the crocus blooms and wild birds sing,
And violets rise from their ancient bed
To feel and touch the pulse of poignant spring.
While she is in this world of springtimes past
She's not alone, for a youthful man is there.
His coming tells her springtime love can last,
Though only she can see him young and fair.
With them are six who prattled at their knees
With cries and laughter that they like to hear,
In their old home beneath age-harried trees.
She sees her violets rise up each year
And crocuses flaunt blooms of windy gold,
Where dream and spring will not let her grow old.

SONGS THAT SING THEMSELVES

Bright July is a month when warm winds rove
Over the green-cloud hills and through the wheat,
Up valleys, through lace fern and bracken cove,
Each puff a sonnet I cannot repeat.
The hungry bees, like fields of Queen Anne's lace
And butterflies, feast on the dusty yarrow;
Their bright wings flash through lazy, sunlit space.
What will they do? Where will they go tomorrow?
Each lonely day she spends is a fickle coin
While stalwart corn turns golden in the furrow.
All fragile life will know when summer's gone
Into bright fields of autumn death and sorrow.
And we who hear these July songs rejoice,
Though poignant lyrics often bring a tear.
The songs that sing themselves have been my choice.
Now we must wait until another year.

BEAUTY FOR US IS THEIR EXCUSE FOR GROWING

The bleak, slick sarvice, bony dogwood trees
Cling on tenaciously to rugged slopes
And show how little food can lift one's hopes.
Their branches are strings for wind threnodies,
Music for a million ears and vibrant tongues,
Music for April life to contemplate
After a winter ruthless, desolate,
April's music to make the aged young!
Wild threnodies before the April showers,
Soft-waking music for the terrapin,
Who breaks up from the ground to join the wind,
What eats the clover but who leaves the flowers.
Trees with so little nutriment have shown
A contribution greater than their being.
Beauty for us is their excuse for growing
On uplands populated with the stone.

IN THE MUSIC OF THE WIND

Life is here,
music is here,
Love is here.
Poetry is here
  in the music
    of the wind
      in the saw-briars
    and the great magnificent sweep
    of the dead leaves
      that cover the earth now.
There are thousands
  of lines
    of poetry
      in the wind here.
It is poetry
  that never grows old.
One only has
  to take a pen
  and copy the melody
    from the wind,
  the words
    from the earth.
It is life here,
Is great life.

ETERNAL HILLS HAVE MUSIC

The whippoorwills, the winds and sheep bells break
The silence of the mountain evenings here.
Breezes among the slick-leafed poplars make
Sweet tunes the outlanders would like to hear.
Sometimes the grunting pig, the mooing cow,
Splinter the glassy silence of the night,
As beetles that groan in the white-top now,
Beneath a canopy of white starlight.
No need to let the lonely whippoorwills
Be all the music on these upland farms,
For there are sheep bells on these sunset hills
When foxes come for lambs to spread alarms.
Eternal hills have music of their own,
The whippoorwill, sheep bells, wind fife-and-drum;
The slow beat of raindrops on leaf and stone,
Eternal music for the years to come!

FROM SPRING TO LEAF-STREWN FALL

Yes, we laugh to the music of the wind
That whines through orchard grasses slow of dying.
We do watch leafless silver maples bend
With their gray fingers clawing wind and crying.
We do shout to dead leaves wind-tremulous
Above the pawpaw paths the cows have taken.
Grain in our stacks, the world belongs to us
From fall of leaf until spring snakes awaken.
Let milkweeds spindle to the earth at will,
And chestnuts trickle from their velvet burrs.
Let farewell-summers shrivel on the hill,
And jar-flies moan from dying grass churr-churrs.
We do shout to the music of it all
From green spring to the glorious leaf-stewn fall.

SING OUT, WILD HEART

Sing out, wild heart! Sing in your windy mood!
Sing to the playful wind. Sing your gay song.
Sing out, wild blood! Sing songs of your wild blood!
Sing loud! Sing gay! Sing! Sing! Go sing your song!
This is your life. This is your native land.
These are your hills, your rivers, and your bottoms.
Sing out your songs, your people, and your land,
Through winters, springs, the summers and the
    autumns.
Sing! Sing of ox carts, wagon wheels, and plows!
Sing of the little world where you belong,
The round-log shacks, cornfields, mules, and spotted
    cows.
Sing, poet! Sing! Sing wildly wild your song!
Remember song was in you from beginning,
Back in your sires in drinking and in sinning.

MAE MARBERRY

A slender child, she gathers flowers today.
She gathers blue sweet-williams from the woods
Where trees are still unleafed and woods are gray.
She gathers wild flowers from these solitudes,
Wind-flowers and blue sweet-williams while she may.
The clouds roll over in the sky above
And winds are blowing 'cross the poplar cove,
And Mae Marberry picks the flowers she loves.
The wind and skies are big, big things to her.
Of wind and fallen trees she has no fear.
White blood-root flowers are a joy to her.
And soon white blood-root petals will be gone
Back to the earth the stems are growing on,
And soon the child will come a woman grown
And gather petals in a silver gown.

WHEN MORNING STIRS

The feather-bed is made for man to lie on
Who's getting soft and maybe money-wise,
Who for the death of sleep forgets the dawn,
And lies when morning stirs with blinded eyes.
Leaves fallen from the trees are bed enough
For man whose blood runs red in every vein.
Or bed of rocks is not too awful rough
With quilts of wind and sleet and snow and rain.
The screech owl shivers notes he loves to hear.
The barking fox is music to his ears.
Of long dark gloomy nights he has no fear,
With brain and flesh well-seasoned by the years.
What are soft beds to him who loves the pines
And feels a brother to the oak and fox?
Who loves the wind that stirs wild-hanging vines
And roar of water splashing over rocks?

BE IN A JOYFUL MOOD

Be in a joyful mood and walk with me
Into beginning spring's cool solitudes
Where streamlets sing so inconsistently
And singing birds are busy in the woods.
All nature now begins to harmonize,
Since percoon eases through the deadleaf mold
To flaunt white banners to the wind-blue skies
In young, strong winds of spring still winter-cold.
The highest mind today is not enough
To celebrate the long-awaited spring
And greet the snowy percoon on the bluff
And watch song sparrows rise and hear them sing.
Our spirits must be high to go and find
Nature's perfection in the flower and tree
And solitude that will inspire the mind
When we are part of all this harmony.

I KNOW A PLACE

I know a place where the wild pansies grow
Among dry chips of cow dung, where sedge vines.
It is the ugliest hill on earth I know.
So poor it only sprouts sedge grass and pines
And multi-colored pansies sweet as light.
When the eyes have been closed all of one's life,
And then the film's removed, with restored sight
He sees the things he touched in his blind world—
Pine needles and petals of pansies curled
Up to the midday sun and browsing winds
And dry chips of cow dung they're growing in.
They are sweet-colored to this earth they're in—
Growing where it was not their choice to grow,
But they give color to this drab I know.

NO SPRINGTIME YET

Wild woodland rose blooms sweetly on this hill,
And down among brown crumbling pasture rocks
So sweetly blooms the pretty daffodil
And fragrant blossoms of the tender phlox.
No land of black oak, sycamore, and pine
And fertile oak-leaf loam of rotted leaves
Can quite compare to rustic land of mine,
White-petaled woodland flowers and deep green
    leaves.
No springtime yet has thrilled the heart of me
As springtime here among Kentucky hills.
No springtime has become such part of me
As dark Kentucky's white spring-splashing rills.
Sonatas of green seas of leaves and grass,
Moonlight sonatas, music not born to pass!

SPRINGTIME KENTUCKY HEAVENS

Forever my blue canopy of heavens,
Color of winds, metal of blue-bowl winds;
Forever my springtime Kentucky heavens
Where gods play *Rights of Spring* on violins.
I have not seen beyond this hallowed land
Of dark Kentucky and her green-vine hills.
Springtime, and I plow her sweet-scented land.
At night I listen to her whippoorwills,
Her streams that tumble over rocks and logs;
Her leaves that catch the wind-blown hair of gods
And whisper like thin voices of lean frogs;
The glistening white spring dew of gum leaf pods.
Forever my white canopy of Heaven
At night with stars, at day with sun, is given.

LIGHT AND SHADOW

Invisible hands are now dispersing dew
On morning-glory bell and buttercup.
Long, unseen arms extend across wind-blue
To gather all the jeweled dewdrops up.
The spiders' silver strands in homes respun
From seeded crabgrass stem to bullgrass blade
Must give their decorations to the sun,
Return the gifts that silent night has made.
And unseen fingers on these hands have found
The baby-handed moles that love the night
And sent them back to holes deep underground.
Moles' little half-eyes were not made for light.
Invisible hands of light have found their own,
Dewdrop and mole and silver strand flower,
Dispersed of all the darkness night has sown . . .
Light over darkness has a final power.

INVISIBLE SLICE OF TIME

Invisible slice of time coloring green,
Moodsong for valley and for rock-capped hill,
This annual resurrection we call April
Is born today amid a winter scene.
Ten million fluffy flakes spiraling down
To cover brownleaf carpet under timber
Is magic April's birth, crows will remember,
With each pine weighted in a snowy gown.
April is born beneath a blinded moon,
This month for great rejoicing and rebirth,
When winter sleepers will rise up from earth
And the worm turns butterfly in its cocoon.
Beginning now, beneath the world's wide rim
The earth will soon be seething at its seams
To resurrect ten billion living dreams!
I will go out and be just one of them.

NO NEED TO MAKE BELIEVE

There is no need to make believe it's spring,
Because the rose in you is shriveling fast.
Pallor is not the green-flush of the spring;
The flush of red-rose cheeks will fade at last.
There is no need to make believe when leaves
Gold as your hair swirl over earth so fallow
And winy wind in berry vines now grieves
And carries leaves red-crimson and light yellow.
There is no need to suffer any change,
But let your body change without a reason
As seasons change and years come swift and strange—
Why fight the ancient gods who claim their season?
Give your beauty; accept the days' declining
As sawbriar leaves fade with the wind's low whining.

URGENT SPRING

Earth's barren face was restless everywhere
On slopes from valley to the high hill's crown,
Until white thread-roots were massaged with care
By gentle rains the heavens had sent down.
Hard kernels fallen from the last year's trees
Awakened to new life with root and leaf,
Since autumn winds had covered them with leaves
Where they could hie away from winter grief.
Earth was awakened by a stirring strife,
May apple's breaking through the leaf-crust mold,
Percoon's soft dreaming of a new spring life,
Wild iris's kissing winds with lips of gold.
Earth has arisen from this restless sleep
And gayly dressed to meet the urgent spring.
In silver streamlets happy minnows leap
And on green boughs the wild birds meet and sing.

AFTER THE SNOW

After the snow we greet the spring with cheer,
Each emerald oak bud and sprig of green;
We greet the little streamlets running clear,
High, rugged hills and valleys in between.
We breathe into our lungs the fresh spring winds
That blow across the young green fields of wheat;
We laugh at spring's rebirth of terrapins
The way they waddle on their scaly feet.
We run, not knowing why we run about
On our eternal hills beneath the sun;
We sing and mock the redbirds and we shout
And rest awhile and then we rise and run.
Life is so full of new blood in the spring,
Life is so full of beauty and of bloom;
Maybe this is the reason why we sing
And run and shout in earth's big spacious room.

THE WIND BLOWS HIGH

The wind blows high tonight—the wind blows strong.
The yellow leaves fall on the Sandy water.
The leaves are grains of meal that sift among
The naked boughs and the buff-colored fodder.
The moon rides high—a grain of yellow dent.
The oak trees rock—the yellow dent goes by.
He smiles at silent fields in half-contempt—
The wind and trees sing him a lullaby:
"Tra-la—tra-la—tra-la—the moon is high.
Tra-la—tra-la—tra-le—the moon is corn.
O corn-moon, do you hear the hunter's horn?
O corn-moon, do you hear the dead leaves sigh?
Tra-la—tra-la—tra-le—tra-le—tra-li—
Tra-le—tra-li—the moon is yellow corn."

CALL IT GOD

Call it God, if you will.
The leafy trees in springtime,
the early meadows,
the old orchards
   white in apple-blossom time,
ridges of green Irish potato vines,
the blue streams
   running between the dark hills,
the lonely sounds at night,
the wind in the oak tops
and the wind playing
   in the dead September corn
and running through the persimmon trees
   on the broken pasture fields.
Rabbits in the dead weeds
and foxes barking
   from the ridge tops at night.
Call it God, if you will.

GOD'S WORLD

I know God is among His windy skies;
He lights the stars and hangs them in his loft.
God is earth's beating heart and lonely cries
Of wings against the wind so swishing soft.
God has pine fingers clawing for the clouds
And makes his silver winds of evening leap
Through verdant vales and dogwoods' white-sail
    shrouds.
God's clouds are many, lazy, wooly sheep
That leave no wool on heaven's brush and briars.
Here in this world God lives and ever shall
As long as soft lamps shed their silver fires
And autumn moons light up the golden pall
And snow-sheets glitter under sandrock sun
And tumbled hills are etched against the skies.
But when God hears spring's lonesome waters run
The April showers are teardrops from His eyes.

HEAR NOW THE WIND

Hear now the wind blow through the black oak leaves.
Swish—swish—oo—oooooooo oo o—swish—swish—
Hear, hear—so solemn how the wind does grieve—
Swish—swish—oo—oooooooooo—oo swish—swish—
Wind running through the green leaves and
     saw-briars
That vine up bodies of the mighty oaks—
Wind playing fiddles in the green saw-briars,
Caressing oak leaves with gentle love strokes,
Out all alone in spacious solitudes—
Out all alone under the starry sky—
And out alone where nettles in dark woods,
Where soft water dogs nod to beetles' cry
And cry of wind among the Plum Grove trees,
Sweeping, sweeping through all destinies.

GIVE ME MY WORLD

Who has walked here before? Turn back the time!
Forget the good hard road! Go back to trails!
Eardrums attune to murmur and the rime
Of buggy wheels, of fences made of rails!
Who would accept asphalt and power thrust
And lightning speed? Seekers who cannot find!
All dreamer pioneers now turned to dust,
Who loved a place, who had a peace of mind!
Turn back the clock, back when I was a boy!
My bare feet touched soft dust where wagon wheels
Ground dirt to silken silt! Ah, what a joy
To know bare foot and dust sensation feels!
Turn back the clock! Turn back the haunting years,
Blue dreamers with eye sockets filled with rain!
Give me my world without the rioters,
A peace in which to live and dream again.

SONNET TIME

Old Moccasin is moved to ecstasy
To write a sonnet on the sparkling sand.
Springtime is here and wind is blowing free;
It is the sonnet form he understands.
He leaves his hieroglyphics there to read
Beside the placid waters onward rush.
Bathed by the sun and wind he pays no heed
To mouthings of the meadowlark and thrush.
Old lizard watches him with half-closed eyes;
It's fun to watch a snake compose a sonnet.
Stirred by earth's heartbeat under lonely skies,
He climbs a dogwood with white blossoms on it,
Looks down onto a world with life a-stir;
At earth more magic than a pleasant dream,
At multicolored wings that slice thin air.
It's time to write a sonnet by the stream.

THESE ARE THE SYMBOLS

These are the symbols of the land I love:
Log cabins on high banks of yellow clay,
A stream of water threading through a cove,
Tobacco barn's slow sagging to decay,
An apple orchard where the rabbits hide
In green-briar clusters in the unkept balk,
A front-yard paling gate that can't swing wide,
Gnarled shade trees where the old folks sit and talk.
These are the scenes embedded in my brain:
The cabin's chimney made of corn-field rocks,
The sunflowers reaching to the window pane,
The garden palings rowed with hollyhocks.
These are the symbols of the land that's mine,
Encircled by hills reaching for the sun,
And friendly fingers of the cliff-grown pine
That swish clean wind where mountain waters run.

THE RED MOON RIDES

And if you could hear the endless chatter here—
if you could see the red moon on the hills
and hear the rumble and the tumble
     of the coaches in the night—
the zoom of the wind
     in the rusted wires and the briars—
and the moan of the engine's whistle—
ah, if you were only here
as we speed over the rough earth
     on a one-eyed train to some destiny—
over the rivers, under the hills,
over the hills and around the hills
and up the valleys—speeding,
speeding behind a mad bench-legged bull
     that stops for a red handkerchief
     and to get a drink of water—
a bull mad and hot and blowing cinders
     into the night—
when over our heads the red moon rides
and the stars twinkle
     over the Kentucky earth.

LOVE-VINE

There are those so analytic
To call the love-vine parasitic,

When garlands of this lovely vine
Around true lovers' necks entwine

To stimulate love's April dream,
Beneath birchshade beside the stream.

Young lovers know this vine can tie
True love as deep as depths of sky.

Then better leave love-vine and praise
Its being for true love always.

A vine so fragile and so fair,
It lives on sustenance from air.

Better young lovers search and find
Strands of its golden hair to bind

Their troths of love, like love-vines be
Securing love eternally.

The World
as Appalachian Desolation

THE PLACE OF DESOLATION

This is the place of desolation here.
The mines have fallen; tracks have rusted red.
The lizards, rabbits, crows are left to care
Where shacks have tumbled and the damp is dead.
Life was once here: one couldn't ask for more.
Mole-men, fat checks, for mining our black gold,
Stepped sprightly all night on the dancehall floor,
Unmindful that tomorrow's camp would fold.
What of tomorrow when there was today?
And hell with those who spoke of waste and sin;
John-L was god who upped their take-home pay.
They whored and fought and drank highridge and
    gin.
Then, unexpectedly, there came the blight,
An economic fungus over all.
There came Depression's endless lonely night,
Recorded by the blacksnake's writhing scrawl.

WE WHO HAVE SAID FAREWELL

We who have said farewell to many friends
Have come at last to find some solace here.
No, not again for us the world's far ends
When we have found the peace of living here.
We love the bleakness of the winter hills
When cold winds of the world howl round our shack.
We love the green of spring with whippoorwills
And growing days of summer coming back.
But, oh, to be beneath the copper skies,
Amid the shocks of copper-colored corn,
And hear above our heads the honking cries
Of wild geese in October sun at morn.
We who have said farewell shall not again,
When last farewells with winter will remain.

WHAT HAS TIME BROUGHT?

Dancehalls to dreamers' feet have long been closed,
And like dancers the halls lie in a heap
Of silent bones now moldered and deposed.
In miners' shacks the snakes and lizards sleep.
The sourwood leaves are colored in April sun,
Gray-colored as cornbush on winter hill.
Among these bones bare creeper vines now run
And winter wind plays with them at its will.
But four decades ago this was the place
Where life was gay for the dreaming sleepers.
Today this is the place where lizard's face
Snaps out for greenflies from the leaf-bare creepers.
Here in this coal-mine camp, they frolicked, fought.
What does it matter now? What has time brought?

THE GONE

November rains downpouring all night long
In silver arrows angling from the sky,
Tapping his roof in a tattooing song—
Above this muffled song he heard a cry.
The sassafras beside the cellar wall
Was giving green leaf dollars to the wind.
Then, there were rising footsteps and their fall,
Of those who had once lived here walking in.
The open fire had shrunk to dying embers
When he switched on the dry electric lamp.
And while he stirred both fire and memories
The rain blew in; his pillow case was damp.
And here before the embers burning low
The cheerful light drove out the dismal gloom.
He sat among them whom he used to know,
For all the gone had gathered in his room.

SLEEP SEASON

Wild roses bloom beside the kitchen door
And thyme climbs up to hide the rotting walls.
Phlox blooms beside the yardshade sycamore
And chinking falls from cracks where lizards crawl.
Old flowers are here; yard trees remain and birds
Return each spring to build in favorite places.
Don't ask me why the wind's soft spoken words
Inquire about the old familiar faces.
They are all gone; the wind has told us so.
Only the image of the dream remains.
The wind has whispered too: "Time is not slow
To rot the walls and break the window panes
And cause clapboards to curl beneath the sun."
Whispers the wind: "They left against their will."
Now, all have gone from here, yes, every one.
Too many are asleep on Plum Grove Hill.

AUTUMN'S DEATH IS ART

These are the first faint tints of autumn surely,
These shocks of fodder in a wind-bent row;
These frosted stems of oozing white-blood pursley,
And golden leaves in yellow sunlight glow.
This is the blood of autumn that you see
In copper wind, in copper earth and skies;
The blood of autumn streaming from the tree
In fluxions red and yellow to the eyes.
Be prayerful now, for death has come to autumn,
This not-strange death so hurting, wonderful,
That colors milkweeds in the Sandy bottom
And causes honey locust beans to fall.
O autumn's death is art and art is death.
Autumn is poetry—wind words are breath.

NIGHT CHILDREN

Men say these are the children of the night,
These mountain men who cannot read and write.
They may not know the ways to shape a world.
They may not know the words when they are traced.
But they remember well the things they've heard
And soon forget the danger they have faced.
Some of these men are children of the sun—
Unnoticed things of earth one could show you,
And how to run your furrows straight and true.
They could teach many how to use a gun—
They are bronze men who have no fear of toil.
Their education is a book of soil—
They are men taught to work and pray and fight.
Let them be children of the darker night.

WE SHALL GO DOWN RELUCTANT

We shall go down reluctant to our dreams,
Remembering days of amber-colored wine.
We shall go down so many shriveled blooms
To supplement the roots of oak and pine.
The songs of sweet discordant winds will move
The ruffles on your dress, your grain-straw hair,
As you reluctant march with your one love
To roomy sequences of darkened air.
And what of it, since we decay by inches?
Once we were proud and laughed at budding spring.
The lips that laughed will soon return to pinches
Of ashy dust that had its youthful fling.
Still spring returns with new wind-songs to sing.
Spring still returns for trees and butterflies.
Spring does return each year to have its fling,
But man sleeps long with cocoon-blinded eyes.

YOU ARE THE LAST

Reach up, my friend, and grab yourself a star
Out in the cool blue yonder over earth;
With eyes of pioneers will you look far
Over land beautiful that gave you birth;
You are the last, son of nonentity,
Thus measured by the reapers now in power.
Your ancestry has died to make us free
But who remembers in this timely hour?
You are the last leaf on an autumn tree.
When you are gone what can the few behold?
Childless you leave no living ancestry
Who pioneered for homes and not for gold.
You are one of the last remaining few
Pioneer descendants who have really made us.
Now in our passing, in our last adieu,
Who are the ones to care and upbraid us?

WINNERS OR LOSERS?

For Time and Place in this remembered land
Where youth departed, heard the wild-bird songs,
Where youth grown old have written on the sand,
Is there one youth to whom this land belongs?
Who grew up here and owns it heart and soul?
His flesh from sustenance from valleys, hills?
It's what he ate and breathed that made him whole.
His songs were cidia, crickets, whippoorwills.
Others have gone into the worlds unknown;
They have been lost to their beginnings here.
Leaving, forgotten as the years have flown,
They know not Time and Place and lonely year.
The rootless go; the firmly rooted stay.
Who are the winners, losers, in this life?
Those who have gone beyond to seek new day?
Or those who stayed to meet their daily strife?

I WOULD KEEP SUMMER LONGER

I would keep summer longer if I could
Hamper the leaves from losing chlorophyll,
Leaves turning, burning in a flaming wood,
Winds rustling golden sails upon the hill.
So unexpectedly came freeze and frost
When our thermometer reached twenty-six
And our late-growing vegetables were lost,
Our hay not cut and in the barns and ricks.
Out on our frosted fields whitefaces lowed;
Stiff frozen grass was not sweet to the tongue;
Our cows bewildered, thinking it had snowed;
Beside their mothers walked the frightened young.
This sudden freeze and frost will paralyze
As we go from short summer to quick fall;
We had the warning but had we been wise
And listened to the wild birds' warning call?

LITTLE GRAY SERPENTINE ROAD

Little gray serpentine Kentucky road
Up Appalachia's slope, where do you go?
Gray serpent crawling up a bone-dry hill
Under October sun and dawn-blue sky,
You leave your summer skin beside you,
Crawling beneath the bushy tough whiteoaks
Whose last sap-blood has redden'd in their leaves,
Hanging to iron tracery that nurtured them
Like people clinging to last days of life.
Cold winter winds will send leaves scurrying
After the frosts have stymied sap-blood flow.
In valleys and on saw-briar slopes they'll blow
Like flocks of birds to ride among the skies,
To sail on avenues of winter winds.
Now little serpentine Kentucky road,
A picture on our Appalachian hill,
A poem here no one has had to write,
Some later date we shall pass here again
When winter winds have shipped the oak twigs bare
And frozen oaks creak in wind-shaken sleep.
Then we will trace you to your hidden lair,
A mountain home where many children play.

FLESH COMES TO THIS

So many nights we've sat and watched the moon
Ride high above this autumn world of gold,
When butterflies were sealed in stout cocoon,
And snakes cold-blooded found a wintry hole.
We heard sharp winds sigh in the graveyard grasses
Where gravestones crumble and the slabs soon rot,
Where bullbats scream in their night fluttering passes,
And mountain people are too soon forgot.
We've loved each other for our little stay
In this gold world beneath such autumn moon.
Our stay can't be forever and one day.
Our lives must break; our lives must break too soon.
Much have we loved and never failed to kiss.
O dust humanity! Flesh comes to this.

O DO YOU WOMEN KNOW?

O do you women know, who lie asleep,
The world moves on and women take your places?
Yes, on and on the world moves while you sleep,
Over your skeleton but up-turned faces.
You helped your husband hoe and husk the corn.
Under the sun you worked, under the moon,
To grow full lines of yellow corn-meal corn.
You bore your children and your rest came soon.
Too soon you were an autumn yellow leaf
Blown out upon the winds of future time.
That prison life for you was almost brief,
Though slow as leaves you ripened into time.
Your dream is silent here among the hills.
You're spring blooms on dogwoods and daffodils.

IF YOU COULD TELL OF WOMEN LONG AGO

You women, too, who lie asleep, I wonder
If you could rise and tell no tales of woe
After the lightning split your graves asunder?
If you could tell of women long ago?
They bore strong sons and you could tell this now,
This dust now sleeping, sleeping on the hill.
They bore strong men to use the ax and cutter plow,
But now these women pioneers are lying still.
They do not hear the zooming spinning wheel,
For those are drifting dead leaves that they hear.
And these are not slim fingers that they feel
Now tangled in their lips, their eyes, and hair.
But those are tiny roots that pierce the ground
Down where a world of dust now sleeps full sound.

KENTUCKY'S NIGHT WINDS

Kentucky's night winds
try to follow the train.
Hear them zoom
   among the rusted wires
   and the saw-briars—
Hear them sweep
   across the hills—
Hear them sweep
   into the night—
mocking the voices
   inside the coaches—
voices of women
talking to each other
and about their children,
their loved ones,
their homes, husbands,
and the women about them.

YOUR TIME TO SING

Sing out, you poet, free as flying leaves
Are free when they fly in the autumn wind.
Sing out, you poet; sing your songs of leaves
That fly as dead thin ghosts upon the wind.
This is your time to sing; there's only one
Time for to sing your song and that is now.
Sing under the bright light of autumn sun,
Of yellow springtime sun behind the plow.
This is your time to sing, while the ox cart
Is rotting in the chipyard and the cattle yoke
Decaying in the woodshed of dry-rot.
This is the time to sing songs of your heart.
You see, America that used to be
Is fading, fading to eternity.

NO WARNING FROM THE WIND

Wind in soap-bellied poplar leaves, I hear
That somber warning in your plaintive song.
Where did you come from? What eternal sphere
To tell our insects August won't be long?
The katydids express their overjoy
Down in knee-high maturing August grasses;
Tree-frogs chant lyrics from their last decoy.
Grasshoppers leap and sing in sudden passes
From leaf to stem in wild frivolity.
These take no warning of the somber wind,
Not when their season's here and they are free
As this green August world they're living in.
No somber August wind can speak to them,
To slow their gayety and stop their dream.

WIND WALKER

Layers of quilts enfold our mountain world,
Crag, crevice, cove, and gray-starved sleepy land.
Lean, hungry, howling mountain wind has swirled
To feather-bedding drifts the snow-white sand.
My highland world is filled with whistling wind
Still stirring fluff above my frozen bed.
I wonder when wind's blowing here will end?
It puts an endless roaring in my head.
The frozen ferns nod stiffly on the bluff.
Tall frozen trees are creaking in the cold.
Crows' trying tyrant winds have had enough,
And one by one the young strays join the fold.
On smooth unbroken snow I leave my trail,
Soon to be covered by the howling gale.

INVITATION

If you should chance to wander lost someday
On paths that lead through mountains near about
And see briar-tangled banks of yellow clay
And have a time of finding your way out;
If you should chance to see upon that hill
Not far from cone-shaped hills, green-clad in pines,
A house with burdock growing at the sill
And in the front a trellis with rose vines,
Come up and say you are a stranger, friend!
Say you are lost on paths in vine-clad space
And you have failed to find your journey's end.
Stay here with us; we shall not fear your face.
We high-hill people squeeze the stranger's hand
And welcome him, a duty that we must.
Stop here when you are lost upon this land.
We'll know if you are worthy of our trust!

HAWK

His wings outspread, buff-colored, black,
His head thrust forward, slightly down,
Legs folded back beneath tailspread,
Flying above the golden corn,
Looking beneath to find a mouse
The color of the autumn corn.

His piercing glassy eyes aglow,
This chicken hawk went gliding down,
A perfect landing, caught his mouse,
Then rose again, his morsel crushed
Within his bone-gray hooked bill.
Winging up steps of fluid wind
To the top branch of a sycamore,
Flapping his wings he had achieved.

Beautiful predatory bird
Taking a mouse from the farmer's corn,
A delicacy for noonday meal.

THE GOLD OF APPALACHIA

These are the golden Appalachian hills
That shoulder to red evening sunset sky;
Fantastic land, a natural splendor fills
Each hungry heart and mind of passersby.
Deep valleys ripen while rich hills unfold
Like steps up to the higher flat and steep;
In autumn Appalachia has the gold,
A richer wealth it would be wise to keep.
Highways, byways are filled with hungry seekers;
Our Appalachia welcomes these and more.
Let them return to be our honest speakers,
Tell of the riches from the deep heart's core.
Better are these who come to share and part
With autumn riches in each eager heart.

FEBRUARY WINDS

The February winds blow white and shrill
Around the flanks of battered mountain ridges.
The wind and earth are filled with piercing chill;
The rabbits hide among the briary sedges.
The sky is ugly and it hangs so low.
This February winter shawl-cloud weather—
Black shawls of sky above the blanket snow—
Has brought us by the fire with heads together.
The wind howls down the chimney and the smoke
Seeps out across the dimly lighted room
As we pile on more wood and laugh and joke.
What do we care for February gloom?
What do we care for blankets of old snow
When violets and bull-grass dream below?

NEVER WAS NIGHT AS BEAUTIFUL

Never was night as wind-swept beautiful!
Blow by them, winds in deep poetic mood!
Go whine among the sedge where cidias lull,
But do not chill poor circulating blood.
Never were they as humble as tonight
To see the beauty only God can own
From everlasting unto everlasting light,
From shining star to petal, lead, and stone.
Winds tell them they are dreamers in this world
That soon must lie asleep until the spring
When resurrected life will be unfurled,
Leaf, bloom, and seed: each hibernating thing!
Winds tell them to enjoy autumn if they must
Since earth must soon collect its rented dust.

OCTOBER'S VOICE

My autumn earth calls me until I go
Obedient to October's lonely voice
Where a dwindling autumn stream is singing low,
Which is the autumn music of my choice.
October calls me to the things I love,
Hot, dry winds tossing leaves in dogwood coves,
To stubblefields to watch cloud shadows move.
October calls me to a million loves.
Among these many loves the weary snake
Hunting a place at last to hibernate
In hole of crawdad, mole rock-crevice, break,
Before untimely freeze decides his fate.
The flying leaves and wings of butterflies,
Lamenting birds that gather for the south
Are loves that bring the quick tears to my eyes,
Songs to my heart and words into my mouth.

HEART-SUMMONED

Sometimes in bonnet that she used to wear
And faded dress by wild-rose brambles torn,
She moves so lightly on her path of air
As she returns a mother to her son.
She does not knock, nor does she come within
To tell me who her new companions are.
She vanishes upon her path of wind,
Accompanied, perhaps, by cloud or star.

THE GREAT
DARK HILLS

Great dark hills
    with life
        among them,
    with death
        among them.
Great hills,
    green
        millions
        of years ago,
    that give us food,
        shelter,
            and warmth
                in life
and take us back
    to their bosom
        in the end.

GIVE ME MY WINTER LAND

Give me my winter land of beech and pine,
Of narrow valley and the frozen stream,
Dark brooding oak broomsedge and leafless vine.
Give me a winter land wherein to dream
In the great white silence where the air's like wine,
Where long icicles hang from the ledge's seam,
Upheavaled white world where the cold stars shine
And long tree shadows break the white moonbeam.

These are the higher hills that hold more snow,
Beautiful, extra, gift of God's white rain;
In soft starlight and brilliant sunlit glow
Ascends to heavens in white clouds again.
Not all of any winter can depart;
I must retain a portion in my heart.

SPIRIT UNDAUNTED

You mothers of the land have met your doom.
Mothers of yesteryears, you sleep at last.
Grass grows above you now; wild flowers bloom.
Birds in productive spring fly over fast.
No one remembers how you followed cattle
And how you used the ax in yesteryears.
No one remembers how you had to battle
To give man birth, you women pioneers.
There were dark lands to conquer, homes to build,
With faith in rifle and your trust in God.
You crossed the highlands, cleared the valley wood,
And you today sleep under this same sod,
While white clouds like feathery flakes of cream
Float in the sky above you and your dream.

REMEMBER KINSMEN HERE

Leave them beneath this mountain.
Their tomb is deep.
And strew wild roses here
Where kinsmen sleep.

Miners, they went beneath
In night-black holes.
Water has trapped them there
And death enfolds

Them in their mining shrouds.
Remember them
Who lie a mile below
In a coal-mine seam.

Remember kinsmen here
In their last sleep.
Go spread wild roses where
Their tomb is deep.

SYMBOLS OF DESOLATION
(Lines for T. S. Eliot)

The crows
  will fly
    over here.
The wind
  will blow.
The rats
  will make
    footprints
      on the logs
and the wind
  and the rain
    will change
      the rat prints.
They
  will smooth
    them over
and the rats
  will make them
    again.
And thus
  it happens
    in the wasteland.

SAY NOT THE YOUTH OF SPRING

Say not the youth of spring will bloom forever
Like white thin petals hanging from the bough.
Say not the birds of spring will sing forever . . .
They'll chirrup lonely on the winter bough.
But say the fine-curved lips will turn to pinches
Of rich white dust to make spring flowers blossom;
Strong bodies will deteriorate by inches
And stalwart trees will spring up from their bosoms.
Say wind will sing forever, for it will,
From earth into the canopy of skies.
New grass will come each spring onto the hill
To give new blooms to swarms of butterflies.
But say not youth in spring will bloom forever . . .
Just springtime once, no more—no, never, never!

RIVER RAILROAD MAN

Shovel under this old river railroad man with
    reverence.
He slept river nights of his life working
After days of work on river railroads.
Now he goes to his long sleep.
Still, heavy trains sweep on to their destiny
For his life is in them and lives.
His blood is in the smoke.
His blood is in the steel.
He heard mean winds strike the cold wiring on zero
    mornings
And whistle through the lonesome treetops.
He heard moaning engines climb steep river grades
And he heard the click of steel battering steel.
Now these same sounds that once he heard
Will continue to whine over his cool tomb
Where he will lie cold
And dream of picks and shovels.

ERODING EPITAPH

He climbed a path where tall, lean, lonesome pines
Shut out the sun above a lichened stone.
Here he deciphered two eroded lines:
The temple rests in earth when it's undone;
The spirit will return to be with God.
Fair land, too often scorched by forest fires,
Leaving a satiny ash on sweetened sod,
Warm, wretched wasteland fenced by wrangled briars.
On shaded stone he sat beneath green skies,
Recounting his days through decades of change.
A lizard looked at him with beady eyes
And then he thought this atmosphere was strange,
That only a free man's dream could be a factor
Supplanting man's croding cpitaph,
Since man and lizard ancient time was after.
So he got up and walked back down the path.

AFTER ANOTHER DAY OF LIFE IS DONE

You thistles, give your sweet blooms to the bees.
You milkweeds, give your cotton to the wind.
You silkweeds, give your nectar to the bees
That weight your blossoms till your small stems bend.
The cowbells slowly tinkle where the quiet
Of uplands spreads toward the set of sun.
They sound so lonely in approaching night
After another day of life is done,
And dew comes to the blades of grass like moons
Set in a bowl of green-grass fluffy sky,
And spider webs are silvered stout cocoons
To trap the lightning bug and little fly—
Soft carpet grass beneath a mellow sky,
And silver threads that hold flies till they die.

AUTUMN HAS PAINTED BEAUTIFUL

Autumn has painted beautiful this year,
Kentucky valleys, coves, and tumbled hills;
The wind and God at work have come so near
Covering the autumn world's deep scars and ills.
This is a world of color to be seen,
Splashes of crimson, black, tarnish, and yellow;
Ox-blood, light-yellow, saffron, spotted-green
On slopes of tumbled hills and old fields fallow.
We know today Death rides the autumn wind;
Beautiful Death is and pulling down the shuttters
And laughing at the world he leaves behind,
And at the goldenrod half-scared that flutters.
The season for all summer fruit is ended.
Then farewell, flowers, in your sweet array.
Rest you in peace, old fields, who have been tended
Too much for your own good in your brief day.

WINTER EDEN

The cold white silence of this winter world
Blankets the brutal scars seared on this land.
Last night the moon looked down on woodlands
    curled
In frosty sleep above the snow-white sand
While men sat back around each log-shack fire
And told their stories of background creation,
While dry foresticks made leaping flames leap higher.
They told of sires who made this land a nation.
The great white silence of our world moved on.
Snow-melted water ran in leaping streams
Down deep ravines to rivers and beyond.
This flowing water took away their dreams.
Now all is still except for wind in pines
And water leaping wildly down ravines.

THE DRIPPING OF THE RAIN

"Tick-tock, tick-tock, tick-tock, tick-tock, tick-tock."
Is that the dripping of the rain I hear?
"Tick-tock, tick-tock, tick-tick, tick-tock, tick-tock."
You never mind the ticking of the clock;
You never mind eternity that's here;
That may be water beating on a rock.
"Tick-tock, tick-tock, tick-tick, tick-tock, tick-tock."
O you blue dreamer sleeping on this hill,
You did not hoard up piles of gold to will
Your sturdy sons before you went to sleep;
You willed more rightful things for them to keep!
You willed them strength to work beneath the sun;
You will them "Will" that's tough to come undone.
You willed them life that is American;
You willed each what it takes to be a man.

LEAVES ARE CLEAN TRUMPETS

Leaves are clean trumpets blurting out Time's noise.
Time can't escape with leaves forever near.
Through lilting leaves of Spring, Time shouts his joys,
But Time moans moodily when they are sere.
Have you not loved the hills in clouds of green?
Looked at the April skies and reached for them?
Threw sticks in splashing runlets there between
These hills that shouldered to the sky's white rim?
Life was before you and your blood ran free.
Life was before you and you were in love
When wind hummed tunes through leaves incessantly
In every hollow and each tiny cove.
You leaped the streams and shouted useless words
Against Time in the leaves and all Time said,
Rejoicing with Time, leaves, and singing birds,
Unmindful that the leaves would soon be dead.

THE DAUGHTERS DEER

Here in October, under yellow leaves
On sugar maple, sycamore, wind grieves.
Stand here where there are skyholes to look through
At white clouds floating on October blue,
While multicolored leaves float on the stream,
Going so far away, so like a dream.
From bank to bank leaves spread across the water,
Propelled by crying winds that follow after.
Laments for long ago is in wind's crying,
Laments for life and for the autumn's dying.

Wind brushes back the trees' disheveled hair
But Charlie Deer's ten daughters aren't there.
Now naught to them wind's sigh and water's moan
And where their dwelling stood the pile of stone,
Where supple poplar saplings like young teens
Reach for the sky but held by loving vines.
Two-story log that skillfully was built
Now has returned as earth's most fertile silt.
Annie and Charlie Deer had built a dream,
Ten daughters in their home above this stream
Now rushing to the rivers and the sea,
Like daughters taken to eternity.

Beneath where their house stood, Whispering Grass
Still guards road ruts where people do not pass,
Where rubber-tired fringed surreys used to roll.
Over the sandy road, through waterhole,
Buggy and hug-me-tight spun down this road.
Mules pulled joltwagons with a heavy load.

Annie and Charlie and their daughters ten
Rested on evening in the cooling wind,
And watched the road to see the people pass;
So whispers to me now Whispering Grass.
Only the sighing Whispering Grass
Here in this great reforested morass
Tells of this family who once lived here
In changing seasons of the yesteryear.

Ten mountain maidens who were filled with hope
In spring watched dogwoods blossom on their slope,
Spring evenings heard the songs of whippoorwills,
Young time of loneliness among their hills.
Ten maidens longed for men they could not blame,
Who saw them walk toward the sunset flame.
Their fondest dreams of marriage were as far
From them as their home was from the brightest star.
Ten maidens' names were written on the water,
Too much coughing with their gay spring laughter.
Death stenciled their names on the April wind;
Once on a sugar maple you would find
Initials of ten daughters on this tree,
Lovers like winds flown to eternity.

Whispering Grass tells me: "Look where you will;
Look for the sugar maple on the hill;
The largest valley tree that ever grew;
Look everywhere." Wind speaks: "The tree's gone
        too!"
Eight-foot diameter, top in the sky,

Valley's most famous tree till death came by,
Uprooted in storm it fell asleep.
A hundred lovers' names its loam will keep.
Initials in its bark have gone to dust;
Like Annie, Charlie Deer's fair daughters must.

Most beautiful brunettes, blue-eyed and fair,
Young men who looked twice, thrice, still were aware
That death had set his mark upon each face.
They coughed too much to share the kiss, embrace.
Their breath held dire contagion, young men thought,
Such disappointment their great beauty brought.
There was no way to counteract the cough.
After "they lingered" death was kind enough
To take each from her bed to final sleep,
On Three Mile Hill, a bed both dark and deep.

But who knows in October of this year
This was the home of Charlie, Annie Deer?
Daughters' home here, in this golden wood,
Upon this spot I stand, where their house stood!
With old friends gone, not anyone knows now
How Annie, Charlie, worked with hoe and plow
To feed their beautiful but lingerin' brood.
The wind today in sad October mood
Speaks to the leaves, and leaves speak to the wind.
Better their love is gone, love once so blind.

Who hears the voices of the long ago?
Who sees fair maidens with their cheeks aglow

Standing with lovers by the sugar tree,
Cutting initials for the world to see?
Young men whose thoughts were filled with a doubtful
  dream
Walked with their lovers here beside this stream,
Heard winds blow over in their autumn clatter:
"Consumptive girls." They knew what was the matter.
Come spring, when oaks had leaves and buds thereon,
Another mountain maiden would be gone
To lie forever on the Three Mile Hill;
Ears deaf to lonely songs of whippoorwill,
Eyes blurred to sight of satin dogwood bloom,
Since she had entered in her quiet room.

Steep slopes that fed them once grow up in trees.
And who remembers now the tragedies
Of life Charlie and Annie Deer once faced?
And broken dreams of men who once embraced
Deer daughters who were fairest of the fair?
Initials on their tree no longer there?
But on the Three Mile Hill a forest grows
Where there are unmarked mounds in unkept rows.
Annie and Charlie and their lovely brood
Lie here beneath the roots of a locust wood.
All said for them will be wind-spoken word
About the beauty that was here interred,
And maidens' dreams of love they never knew
Beneath the yucca sparkling in the dew.

WHEN WE DESTROY EARTH WE HAVE THE MOON

I

Securely belted on this jettified bee,
Looking down on mountains of West Virginia
From this small plane embattled by the wind,
Beneath are places I don't want to be.
Down there, monster manmade machines are
    crawling,
Rending rind and ribs into the bowels
Of mountains folded by the hands of God.

II

The long gash wounds show on the flanks and tops
From foothills up to where the tree line stops.
These raw rind wounds have never been sewn up
For they lie open and the blood runs yellow,
Down over wrinkled skin that's dark and fallow.

III

Wounded mountains, what is your destiny?
Lie there while your eroding wounds get deeper
In land where man has been a century sleeper.
Will they be healed by reawakened youth?
Will they be left to be healed naturally
And leave your tops and flanks with ugly scars
Illuminated by the sun and stars?
Now you lie painfully in winter sun
Divided by valleys where swift rivers run,

Rivers of silver ribbons from this stair
To make a net that cannot hold your wind,
But can hold dark pine forests of your hair.

IV

Ah, land once beautiful beyond compare,
Important, mountainous West Virginia,
That is a part, a Principality
Of Fifty Grand that make America;
A Highland Principality up where
Destroyers gouge mountains unmercifully;
Where they are not required to heal your wounds,
Where they are free as they were yesterday
To wound again and watch you bleed to death.
Does it mean naught to them if you should die
When to America and to the world
You can be beauty and a joy forever,
A beauty resurrected to the world?

V

I must remain in this jettified bee
And glide above you faster than the wind,
But slower than the dazzling sun's rays dart
Behind, between, and over and around
Multicolored cloud-ranges up here now
And valley meadows with all blossoms white
With night cloud-ranges ambered by the moon.

VI

Narrow-gauged valley lying below,
Houses alike, two rows from thigh to toe;
Narrow-gauged valley with a winding river
And parallel to it a snake-curved road.
And now down there is where I want to go
Among disturbing gash wounds on the mountains,
Where mountain blood comes down in yellow
     fountains,
For sleepers failed to close these ugly wounds.
They let wounds bleed where there black gold
     abounds.

VII

Mountains, you have my sympathy down there,
You wounded monsters lying in the sun
Where cruel elements can't heal your wounds.
Unhappy mountains with your beauty marred,
A scenic wealth once greater than black gold,
Green scarless splendor that you used to wear,
Search all the fifty principalities
And their component parts will not compare.
If healed again your beauty will enfold
These bleeding scars of where you found black gold.
World travelers and Americans will see
The Principality you ought to be.

THE LAND CRIES FOR THE TREES

The land cries for the trees to come to it,
To hold the skin of land in its right place.
But ghosts of trees cannot return to land.
For railroad cinders to a shady place,
Where there is music in the blowing wind,
And beauty in the roof of changing skies,
Where there is sustenance for tree roots in
The soft loam where worms work in paradise.
But they resign to earth to grow again
And drink once more of gentle springtime rain,
To grow again up from the graves they've left,
From valley to thin-dirt on sandstone cliff.
For trees, like men, have suffered misery
In exploitation's reckless destiny.

The World
as Ship of State

TWO KINDS OF YOUNG BIRDLANDERS

In our Birdland we birth millionaires
In ghettos and the better neighborhoods;
They're birthed in storms, fair weather, day and night;
They're birthed the same as other ordinaries.
When one is born not anyone can say
He will be heading for a million plus;
We must be given time to see him grow
To six-eleven, seven feet, and more,
And have agility for his great height,
Be durable to dribble, spin, and shoot
Or lay the basketball up in the hoop;
Then he'll be scouted with sharp eyes on him.
Bids will go to a million, maybe more;
New home provided for his family, too,
For millionaires have their society.
Maybe the bid will reach three million plus;
Such a man will have respect, a household name,
And be a hero to Birdland's millions.

Other young Birdlanders will live in attics,
Pore over day and night their compositions,
Music created to last for centuries;
Stay in their attics, write immortal books.
Go to the attic, paint a famous picture,
Sell for a million when the artist's gone.
These young creators will, in native Birdland,
Go hungry on their little gifts and prizes,
They with immortal names in Birdland's future.

A million now is far beyond their dreams
Since they have not been birthed as millionaires;

While all the basketeer will have to do
Is pace the hardwood on big feet and shoot
And steal the ball and throw it through the hoop.
Unfortunate for the multitude of males
Not to be born with great agility
And grow skyward, stalwart, seven feet tall,
Run fast, have sense enough to handle the ball.

PRECIOUS TV

Yes, this beginning of another year
Our twenty-five super-dupers are here,
These twenty-five favorites now proclaimed,
These egotists, our favorites, are here
On favorite media, precious TV,
Which is our nonessential and time-waster
Where spiritualistic favorites play
With too-familiar faces day on day.

You in the future time to come should see
Our twenty-five esteemed and lovely faces
With us today in popularity for a time,
Tomorrow left without poetic rhyme.
What these would do to you we'd like to know,
If they would make you cry and dance and sing,
Or do a flip or do your future thing!
But you will know what they have done to us
On our time-stealer in our idle hours.
Murder and rape have been our daily diet.
Fed to us with a spoon until we accepted
These entertainment theses with sheer delight,
We with the highest crime rate in the world.

THANKS TO TV

Life began two hundred million years ago,
Warm water in rivers, oceans, ponds, swamps,
Announced by a Savant over gospel-truth TV,
Which will arouse, awaken, shake, bewilder
Millions of our two-hundred-millions plus,
Whose education prepared them to believe
That there was void and darkness on the deep.
And out of this deep darkness came a world
Created in six days and on the seventh, Sunday,
Our earth's Creator took a day of rest
For overwork had made him very tired.
Therefore, forever after, Sunday is
The day of rest for all the faithful ones.

Conceive two hundred million years ago,
Which is a very short time for beginnings
According to our immortal TV's
Authoritative Savant on all unknowns,
Communicative genius of images
Predicting time from fossils, stones and bones.
Remember, TV is to be believed!
You had better believe it is believed!
Now sitting here until my TV fades,
Replaced by mystic primeval light,
A prehistoric world goes back to dawn,
Mists rising from the waters up in clouds,
Flora, fauna, gigantic animals
Eating in eerie light, leaves from strange trees,
Little forelegs, long tails, and little heads,

Long limber necks, maybe predinosaurian;
Stud terrapins as big as bungalows,
Reptilians log-size on water, land,
And monster lizards scaling over sand
And flying bats with three reptilian heads;
Young world to give hallucinatory visions
So pleasing, entertaining to the senses.

Thanks to TV's authoritative Savant,
Old Knowledgeable on the Master's seat,
Long hair and beard and a doodledo-bird suit,
With one brain less than primeval Dinosaur
(Who had a small brain in his little head
And a smaller one down in his massive rear,
Two brains put Dinosaur in Special Class),
Imparting knowledge to the uninformed,
To poor down-trodden nonreading people
Now reaching for the Higher TV Light.
Thanks for visions in primeval mystic
Sights but not sounds always to be remembered.
Thanks for a look into my world's beginnings,
That sharpies on TV have commandeered,
To show us how we got the world we have,
A world of lust and greed and seedy sinning.

DENO OF BIRDLAND

What's happen'd to Hero Dean Martin?
We've not seen Dean's likeness for months
On our immortal TV screen . . . .
Spirited Deno known for cavortin',
Great "Hero" on American earth,
A money man, superb prestige,
A thriller, chiller, killer in
Our Great Birdland's Golden Age.
Deno's in balance on the ledge,
A most important actor, sage!

TO A BUZZARD
(Circling Low Over the Capitol,
September 8, 1945)

Tell us. What do you want, giant scavenger,
Invading fruitless skies?
                              You're far from home
Here over Washington!
                              Have you no fear,
Your wing-tips fanning our capitol dome?
Bird of your ilk was never known to search
For beauty of such fascinating kind
At a citadel where blue-blood pigeons perch!
Tell us, you daring bird, what's on your mind?

What do we have appealing to your passions
To make you brave the traffic of our air?
It could not be that you are scarce of rations,
That you have come expecting us to share?
Go, uninvited guest! Leave us forever!
Your coming here is most embarrassing!
We could not welcome you, no never, never. . . .
Shoo, bird!
                              Your presence is an evil thing!

THE PRESIDENT AND I

My son, my son, why have you run so fast?
Each breath you take comes harder than the last.

I sent you to the cattle-pond tonight
To see if thirsty cattle were in sight.

You came home running faster than a rabbit!
I know, my son, running is not your habit.

What made you run? Still almost out of breath
You are as pale now as a corpse in death.

Did someone follow you with a big stick,
And did you accidentally catch a lick?

Stop asking, Father, now my breath is back,
And I'll tell you what made me ball the jack.

Our herd had come for water to the pond
And I was there to count the sixty-one.

The full moon rose up like a wagon wheel;
Our pond was light from valley to the hill.

My son, you've seen the moonlight on the water,
And you have heard night winds' incessant laughter;

And neither of these made you run before,
And fall death-pale and breathless in the door.

But Father, Father, give me time to tell,
Now I have breath, what made me run like hell.

I saw him walking upright on the water,
Out there alone and no guards chasing after.
The only sound was night winds' liberal laughter!

You mean, my son, you saw the living God,
Who left no water footprints where He trod!
My son, if you have seen the living God,
O, O, my son, I'll say it's very odd!

How could your human eyes focus His light,
Brighter than stars on the milky way at night?

No, father, no . . . I saw our President,
He walked and left no tracks the way he went;
He walked, his head was bowed, his back was bent!

I stood and watched. I saw him raise his head.
And then I wondered if I might be dead,
A spirit in our future world of bliss;
Our President and I had come to this.

Then, suddenly I felt my body burning;
Like a fox I ran, my legs like pistons churning.

Our run-down barn, our run-down granary.
Night wind sighed: "Poverty, O poverty!"
The crying, sighing night wind spoke to me.

With less farm work and no more drudgery,
Maybe no work, and sure no poverty,
He walked on water now to set us free,
Our own, our dear, beloved Lyndon-B.

My son, my son, don't spread this to the Nation.
It's mockery, your big hallucination,
Vote getting as contagious propagation!

They'll say something's the matter with your mind;
Some ill a good psychiatrist will find!

Father, you think I've cut a crazy caper;
I've seen his million images on paper

And on TV and on the movie screen;
Each step he takes I know where he has been.

I know his turkey neck, his turtle lips,
Tall man with a long arm and big hand that grips

The voters' hands with all his good intent.
Do you think I don't know our President?

Father, I know I saw him walking on
Wind-ruffled waters of our manmade pond,
The Government helped us financially on.

O, father, father, do you understand?
He walks on water same as on the land.

Father, are you too old to realize
That in his photos stars are in his eyes?
Of all our Presidents he is the prize.

I know I saw him walking on our pond,
And who would know where he has walked beyond?

Maybe into our future world of bliss
But now he has no reason to do this.

He's King on Earth where he is reigning now,
Created wealth without sweat of the brow,
A formula our kings have missed somehow.

Father, I know the night wind sighed to me:
"Never again will there be poverty."

With big soft words and gestures of the hand,
All poverty is banished from our land,
Forever from,
        Forever from,
           Our land!

SWILL SOCIETY

Swill soaking now has its
Great popularity,
New fad in Washington,
Swill from the Federal till.
In our America
You bathe in Federal swill
From crown of head to heel.

In Cleopatra's day
Sweet Lotus-bloom perfume
Swayed their Society
In bright feluccas on
The old enchanted Nile!
Breathing this sweet perfume
The high Pharaonic Cast,
Lured by Cleopatra,
Most beautiful Queen
The world has ever known,
Swayed Emperors and a world,
Yet not comparable
With swill soaking today,
Millennia hence in our
Beloved Washington!
Now, Cleopatra and
Her suitors have gone to dust!

First there were thousands in
This great American sport.
Now there are millions more

And millions more to be
In Swill Society!
Swill soakers are in classes
And Swill Class levels are
Ten thousand up to higher
Stratas: sometimes, a million,
Like rose-scented water
In Rome's most glorious baths
On famed Palatine Hill.

Swill soakers cannot live
Without the Federal swill.
They relish atmosphere
In our great Washington
More than lotus perfume
Pharaonic Egyptians loved,
More than rose-scented water
In pink-shell Roman baths
On famed Palatine Hill.
Our greatest luxury will
Surpass these and all others,
Swill soaking in
Beloved Washington!

YOU ARE WRONG
WHEN YOU SAY IT

You are wrong when you say it,
Wrong if you even think it.
I won't suffer in hell
For what I've said about
Viet Nam Nineteen Sixty-six
And our aggressive wars
And our One-Party System.

Someone, I tell you, will
Remember me years hence,
I think, and I'll be saved
By the judgment of good men,
I who have been oppressed
By the fear of oblivion.

UTOPIAN TEMPO
(January 24, 1966)

What will we do
Without a war?
How can we stand
Our emptiness?

No shooting, dying,
No pools of blood,
Stagnation's dark,
Sadistic mood!

All we need now
Is elbow room
And leadership
To break this gloom.

Who can stand life
When it's a bore
And question not
What we live for?

Repulsive is
This quiet life
Too many seek
And men call Peace.

OUR MODEST, CULTURED, ENGLISH COUSINS

Greater than Jesus Christ, the Beatles say,
Greater than His Apostles with thick heads,
More popular than our Christianity.
Why this comparison?
                              Go ask the Beatles!
These long-haired rock-'n'-rollers, English-given,
Come captivating "cultured" screaming youth
Over our land worn weary of its wars.
First in America they made their million
And rose to heights in popularity,
Were wined and dined as heroes of the hour!
Astute publications gave them space that
Our starving attic cats, who write great books
And symphonies, who paint some masterpieces,
Will never get in a lifetime struggle here!
But these sensational, long-hair'd, jazzmen,
Our modest English-given country cousins,
"Blob-blob, flap-flop," bring their great culture here,
Screaming hysteria so pleasant to the ear!
How can we wonder why all others think
Money is all we offer on this earth?
Can we remain the self-styled guiding light
To help our neighbors through approaching night?

WHO ARE THE WINNERS?
WHO THE LOSERS?

Fifty thousand, perhaps more, sensible youth
Defected to a country that would have them;
Yes, wrong or right in that insensible war,
Seventy thousand dead, two hundred billions,
A war we did not win but only "drew."
And should we be patriotic or honest?
Heart-searching decision is up to us!
Tell me, who are the winners and the losers?
My heart aches for my country's deadly sin.

I'm patriotic and American
But I, as sure as hell, cannot agree
To these Democratic wars in my lifetime,
Purposeless wars that have not solved a thing.
For my first time I have not only believed
But I know deceased Charles Lindbergh was right.
Forgive me, Creator of this Universe,
For criticizing this man in World War II,
In which I served, for all I said about him.

I'M NOT YOUR HERO!

I'm not your hero, nor your "thing"
But I do know what our wars bring.
Woodrow's for World Democracy;
This World Democracy my foot!
I've traveled on six continents;
I've seen the countries and the hell
Reaped by the peoples and their dead.
I served F.D.R.'s war to make
Giant friends into our enemies
And our war enemies our friends!
War to end aggression—how noble!
And how insane! The people know!
Our Harry's war, atomic bombs,
Used first and only time in war,
To kill a half million innocents.

And for our dear old L.B.J.!
And for our dear old L.B.J.!
Two hundred billions Vietnam costs;
Seventy thousand lives we know;
And still no win, hardly a draw,
Inflation, world millions hating us!
Do we approach sensibility?
Do we approach civilization?

SYNTHETIC HEROES

When I look on these cheap synthetic heroes,
These little self-importants of our time,
These do-do Birdland Birds, self-styled heroes,
These high-paid heroes in America's news,
I turn to memories of saner days,
Of what was once a more substantial time,
Solid American cultural scene.
With these synthetics guiding us, what will
America be in our continuing?
In years to come many will never know.
But to our American youth we'd better throw
The challenge high to guard against synthetics;
America, in weakness, so pathetic,
Soft ending to what once was strength and now
It's degradation in this future hour.

TOYOKO MINOWA
(A Hiroshima Maiden)

In Hiroshima, you were there,
Survived our holocaust of fire;
You were eighteen and beautiful,
The zest for living your desire.
You made no war; you were the pawn,
A victim of our King's decision!
So helpless then, now twenty years
And forty operations later
You're still alive to show your story.
Our Little King destroyed you;
And he, too, lives, conscious of flame,
Conscious of death he soon must face
And Nether World to which he will
Not take his Presidential Glory.
A Hero here to some, who has
Made ashes of two hundred thousand,
Earth's Number ONE Incineration.

Unlisted infamy dates, our
War Hawks consider Memorable:
August Sixth, Eighth, Nineteen Forty-five!
Erupting Mount Vesuvius,
Pompeii, Herculaneum, Stabil
Destroyed by hot volcanic ash,
One tenth the loss of our two bombs!
Pompeii is only secondary!
And we, those gentle Doves of Peace
With bloody flags out in the wind

Where people still have eyes to see,
Voices to speak and pens to write,
They still want life, not total night.
They still have minds and they can think.
We do not have to think for them!
The old remember, too, that smell
Of burning human flesh caught in
Their nostrils and inhal'd, exhal'd.
This is a memory that's fix'd
To linger till death takes the bearer.

Ah, kill me if you dare before
I go on record with my thoughts;
Grave troubles in my heart and mind
About what guilt I have to share
And darken'd shroud I have to wear!
Around this world I've been accused
By voices from so many lands!
Now twenty years away, our deed
Still fresh in all their memories,
And how could I to them confess?
I'd no part in kill-wantonness.
But like the guilty I must share,
And all our people have to share
This guilt; war won't let us escape!

Is there a future mankind peace,
No spill of blood to crimson land,

A peace the peopled world may share?
Let would-be warring leaders fight
Each other in World Colosseum,
Their weapons being deadly clubs.
Charge modest fees to see this bout.
Let those war advocates kill and
Be killed, while world spectators shout!

Our Little King who gave "the orders"
Would have fought well with a deadly club,
But now he's old and near the grave
And "fire hallucinations" shake him
At midnight in his easy bed.
Until awaken'd he does not know
If he's one of the darken'd dead!

Who envies him his little fame,
This hollow nothingness of fears,
Gossamer sheet of darken'd wind
To camouflage his funeral bier?
When world historians record
This bloodless record of our killer,
Cold killer of this heartless age,
Can we invite earth to forget?
His sin besmirches us like smog
And we can't purify world air.
We live in shadow of this cloud
That wraps us like a funeral shroud.

MICHIKO YAMAOKA
(A Hiroshima Maiden)

How strange you're living in this hour,
Crawling that day to the beach to die;
Now twenty years, eight operations,
You are alive to tell your story;
So badly burned, you have not married.
How you came through our holocaust,
You who were baptized by our fire,
Known to the world as a massacre!
For this we can't apologize;
The guilt lies on our conscience
And lies forever heavy there,
A scrutiny for youth unborn.
Thus we have sinned without excuse.

Your Mother found you on the beach,
So, foreordained you did not die:
This, Michiko, for a noble purpose;
Your living will save millions more!
Now we would like to be your friends
For sense of guilt is unforgiving
And pomp of power is destruction.
Reckless abandon with fire power
And our guilt-stain should show the world!
But will it? Thus, let us be first
And only one to devastate
My Brothers by our hell-inferno!
Michiko, people weep for you!
Not all of us condoned this act;

We too have lost in war's blood letting.
We ask: *What was it all about?*
Unwed, you with your battle scars
Encounter still the searing flame!
And he who gave the orders lives!
No wonder Youth rise here today
To demonstrate against this thing!
No wonder Youth rise up to challenge
One Party's ruling of this Land!
In what direction have we gone?
Have we marched on the road to Hate
Like darken'd figures of the dead?
As fixed in minds around the world
Not all deserve this mark of guilt!

Michiko Yamaoka, you are
Left to live to show our sin;
You cause our Youth to rise and challenge.
You cause some elders like myself
To have faith in a better world.
Tomorrow's Youth we hope and pray
But not our Bird Kings of today!
May we have leaders to thwart
Our lives made dark by sense of guilt
With new respect and love again
Among our neighbors of this world!

SUZUE OSHIMA
(A Hiroshima Maiden)

So badly burned when you crawled home,
Your father did not know his daughter.
Said he, "Whose girl are you, poor thing?"
Now twenty years, ten operations
(You measure Time by operations),
Married you are, mother of two
Nice, healthy children, six and four.
A miracle has come to pass,
Husband, atomic bomb victim,
Birth, atomic incineration!
Though badly scarred, life has been kind;
Our fire did not put out your eyes.
Despite your burns, you have found Love,
This greatest word in any language,
Found more than Hiroshima sisters
Who have been burned beyond desire
And who will work all of their days.
Our thinking people who have cared,
And who denounced this monstrous act,
Are branded radical, some jailed;
Those with right hearts must suffer hell.
We have not learned. We fight today
Upon an endless battlefield.
Our fighting is continuous.
Before eyes of the world we pay.
Today you live, Suzue Oshima,
To show your story to the world,
Blind to realities we face,

(Maybe we lack heart-conscience).
Uncertain years out there ahead,
We've learned we cannot buy this world,
That human flesh, blood, spirit, mind
Are higher than finance's reach.
We have not learned the greatest word
In other languages is Love.
Love's application can change us
And change our enemies for Peace!

You bathed in fire, Inferno-Hell,
In war and hate we thrust on you,
When you were innocent sixteen,
Age of our daughter's living youth.
You have survived to meet New Life,
To see us waste in our new wars,
Late ones; we question what they're for!
A war of purpose we would fight,
Hold grounds or meet an endless night!
We cry aloud how great peace is
When peace is up to us to have!

Romans were honest: they sought war.
And we cry Peace but we fight Wars.
Today Rome has Palatine Hill,
A Hill once powerful and great,
The richest Hill in all the world,
A world obedient to its commands.
Today it's home for owls and bats;

Stones there disintegrate to dust.
Old edifices of rich and great,
Time will take from the tourist's eye.
Today we have Capitol Hill,
Another Hill known to the world,
The symbol of a mighty Land.

Your Hiroshima is rebuilt.
Clean City, new, its past is dust.
Aggressive war there is no more!
No more you will police the world!
But what about our Capitol Hill,
Agressive symbol to the world,
To friends and enemies alike
Who measure us by daily actions?

Palatine Hill's oblivion
Is symbol for an Empire gone,
Wasted in war, corruption, lust,
Riotous living. O why must
We return to Capitol Hill?
Is it, too, symbol of decay?
Will the winds of loneliness someday
Blow here and sing a lonesome song
For wealth and power that have been?
Will birds and bats have final sway,
These playthings on a lonesome wind
That care not what we might have been?
Can we revert to Peace and Love?

Peace for the World to save ourselves?
The pomp and power of yesterday,
Wherever found, led but one way.
Led to destruction and the grave!
If our beloved Land we save,
A path of Peace we must approve
And live eternally with Love!

MISAKO KANNABE
(A Hiroshima Maiden)

Youthful sixteen when you crawled home
Unmindful what had happened there;
At home, no medicine, no doctors!
Firebreaks you were to make, not needed;
You saw your world go in a flash.
Your Hiroshima in ash and dust,
Its stones were pulverized by fire
Intense enough to burn your earth!
Now after twenty years of surgery
You live to say: "The bad is war!"

Misako, you're now beautician,
Denied your normal youth and beauty.
Still you make others beautiful
By working six twelve-hour days
And spending Sundays home relaxing.
Marriage, you know, is not for you,
For plastic surgery leaves scars.

Misako, you will remember
Rubble where Hiroshima stood!
You will remember dust and ash,
Alive, breathing, dreaming, knowing
You'd spoken to that fatal day.
Dust now, your relatives and friends,
In silken ash for winds to lift
Cremation over earth and seas.

This miniature devastation
Of what could come to all the earth;
Misako Kannabe, we wanted
To show our Russian friends our power.
We trusted them, our ally, friend,
Less than we trusted enemies.
We were and are afraid of Russia,
And try to be their bosom friend!
And still our friend has never dropped
Atomic bombs on any city!

We stand alone to bear this guilt,
A darkening shroud enveloping
Us where we go upon this earth!
The voice of justice never dies.
Should we who kill taste death for death?
If death by fire should we feel flame?
Would this remove from us our shroud?
This curse of guilt forever on us?
We hear your dead sing their paeans;
Your darkened dead sing victory songs!

We knew the power of our bomb.
Why devastate the innocent
Of any city? A lesser sin,
Why not select a smaller city?
There is no logic we can use
To clear our conscience for this deed!

We tyrannized your helplessness.
Will this be watered by our tears?

From Hiroshima comes the word,
From grains of dust assembled there.
Better if we speak softly now
And not arouse your spirited dead
For they might come to stand beside,
To weep tears that are never dried,
To know we wear this shroud of guilt
Before the peoples of the world.
We did not bathe you in your blood
When we incinerated you.

World Justice has held high the road,
Assisted by the hand of God,
To those we think met total night,
Crushed by the enemy of right!
Our War Hawks did this thing to you
And the world holds us responsible!
We wonder how you can control
The bitter hatred in your soul!

CAN YOU BE BLAMED?

Can you be blamed for what you did?
You came to earth not by your choice.
If you had known and had your choice
Would you have been a Bird in Birdland?
Would you have come into this Age
Of Local, State, and Fed Wind-Birds?
This Golden Age for Status-Birds?
No wonder you became confused!
Psychiatrist couldn't bring you back.
You did your best with what you had;
You tried in vain to stem the tide
Of Life's Mad River of Confusion.
More fragile than the average man
You didn't shirk responsibility.

Your parents did all they could do.
Your teachers helped you all they could.
Your minister worked hard and prayed
To break down those offensive walls
You thought were holding you within.
Bird Age you never understood.
Caught in the current of Mad River,
You could not swim in its confusions.

Money to you was never God.
You cared not for the right connections:
Commercial birth, commercial death,
Commercial all between these two.
And when you read that coffin ad,
How bedded down in silken silk

In the greatest coffin ever built;
How you could sleep forever in
Such everlasting peace and comfort
And need no more the daily wages
You made by bucking rivets with
Airhammer at the railroad shops.

Five undertakers in your county
Competed for you in the end,
Had advertised for you in life
And this is why that coffin ad
For you to meet eternal peace
Away from all turmoil and strife
Impress'd you at a certain time.
Why should men question now your act,
Respected citizen you were?
Commit this crime to shock your friends?
Why was the life you took your own?
Murder this poet can't condone.

Bird Laws, elastic to the core,
Will not, cannot do anything.
Can they undo what has been done?
How will God's Divine Laws react?
You took a life which was your own
And this was murder! Why would you
Commit such act? You can't hear me
But I am one who puts no blame
Upon you under circumstances;
That in your hour of desperation,

Your seeking truth you could not find,
A way to freedom in Birdland—
Mentally disturbed, you found that ad!

Who wrote this thing to sell a coffin,
This pleasant ad to end all worries
With Peace and Comfort in the grave?
You put the cold revolver steel
Against your temple, pulled the trigger.
This was the only way you found
Certain escape. You paid with all
You ever really owned, your life!

No one found any sin in you.
You worked to live; you owed no man.
Surely God has a place for you
Since you were not received too well
Where you did not request to come;
Relaxless Land, a number Land
That was for you depressive hell
With walls around to shut you in.

Had you but waited for a heart
Attack, a few more years to fell you,
This crime would not be left with you.
Hindsight is better than foresight,
Ancestors say, but is it always?
What can be wrong with your escape,
Strange journey to another world
In search for what you found not here?

AMERICAN WOMEN

American women, if they could speak
From under dirt, from under thin-blue moons,
From under sky and drips of rain that leak
In cells made tight as butterflies' cocoons,
I think these mothers of the land would tell,
"This is the last page of our destiny.
See, here is mine and there is your small cell
Beneath the roots of rose and cedar tree.
Turn pages of this book; I think you'll find
We were like you once, flowers in the wind.
Young women of the land, why not be gay?
One life to live; you only live today.
Go out and live, you young untimely blooms;
Go out, you young wild woodland flowers.
Live in this world and in this time of ours;
For soon, too soon, you will sleep in the tombs."

BELIEVERS

But, since you dreamers cannot speak to me,
I shall pause on my path to speak to you:
You mothers of a nation silently
Now sleep where words cannot leak down to you.
But only roots of corn pierce down to you—
The roots of corn, the roots of brush and trees,
Where rain and snow and leaves blow down to you,
You feel the roots and hear the sounds of these.
You mothers of sons of this infant nation,
We used the cornfield hoe, gave children birth;
Believers you in beauty and creation,
Believers you not in the dollar's worth;
Believers you in individual worth,
Believers in the nation you gave birth!

LOWLY AND ALL ALIKE

Lowly and all alike: the rich, the thief,
The man of fortune and the man of fame,
The farmer, merchant, virgin, and the whore,
All come to dust and dust without a name.
They are all going, going, going, going
Across this broad expanse of destiny;
Going, going, like an ill and fair wind blowing,
Across this stage for man to some eternity.
And why is it we doom our fellow mortals,
Tramp them into the dust because we can,
Treat them as we do snakes, our fellow mortals,
And then say we are good Americans?
We are all children under that big sun;
When that sun sets our travail will be done.

ONE TIME TO SING YOUR SONG

Sing out, you poet, free as flying leaves
Are free when they fly in the autumn wind.
Sing out, you poet, sing your songs of leaves
That fly as dead thin ghosts upon the wind.
This is your time to sing; there's only one
Time for to sing your song and that is now.
Sing under the bright light of autumn sun,
Of yellow springtime sun behind the plow.
This is your time to sing while the ox cart
Is rotting in the chipyard and the cattle yoke
Decaying in the woodshed of dry-rot.
This is the time to sing songs of your heart.
You see, America that used to be.
Is fading, fading to eternity.

The World
as Journey
to Ephesus

JOHN AND EPHESUS

Saint John, we can't forget your grave in Ephesus,
For we were there when your dust was still in the tomb.
Naomi, my wife, world traveler, always with me,
Lover of Ancient Cities, ruins, and antiques.
Told by the guide on our first visit to Ephesus,
Your head was severed and was buried elsewhere.
You have to be important in your day and time
To have received such recognition after death,
You, Saint John, disciple of God and Jesus Christ,
A citizen once of the beautiful Patmos,
Where you wrote *Revelation,* the most discussed
And hardest to understand book in our Bible.
Now, we've returned to Ephesus, our favorite
Nonexisting city, place of dry bones
Where a disturbed wind constantly hums ditties
Along the Great White Way; the street where ancients
    walked,
Dramatists and poets, including Saint Paul and you.
Would not we now, two thousand years and flying
    oceans,
Have liked, Saint John, to have seen you in this city
Walking along the Great White Way with guest, Saint
    Paul!

Later your tomb was opened and, maybe, your dust;
Reports say pieces of bone, as well, were taken to
    Rome.
Why take your dust to Rome? Why not leave your
    dust in

Your tomb, so near your church in native Ephesus?
You had a beautiful tomb where we are standing now,
Where thousands come, fellow Christians, Moslems,
    Jews.
Two summers past we stood here near your dust in the
    tomb,
With new guide now. A Turkish lady with black eyes
Explained your tomb contained not your immortal
    dust.
She could have been Moslem, or maybe she was
    Christian.
Christian or Moslem, she was interested in Saint John!
Saint John, you are one of the Moslem Prophets now.
Moslems, they are akin to Jews, whom they so hate,
And Christians are so tied to Jews in their great faiths.
All worship the same God; three great religious faiths
And yet these people should not be so far apart.

Something about your Ephesus is empty, Saint John,
Perhaps because your hallowed dust has gone from
    here
And empty is your tomb where people come and
    stand.
So what stirs in their minds is anybody's guess!
Buried in faraway Ephesus, costal city,
Bemoaned by these incessant Mediterranean winds—
Maybe they blew from Patmos, where you dreamed,
    Saint John;
Where you wrote for the billions in the future world.

At Ephesus' Greek Theater, along the Great White
    Way,
Many a time you sat on one of these stone seats.
You sat on one of these stone seats I've seen today,
Seeing the Great Greek Dramas with your close
    companions;
Maybe with Paul, perhaps with Mark and Luke around
    you.
Birds of the early Christian feather flocked together.
Perhaps the Dramatist, after the play, came back to
    greet you.
Remember, there were stirring times back in your
    days,
In your great city where two million Ephesians lived.
I would have liked to have walked on your Great White
    Way
With you and your companions, have heard your
    conversation,
And to have heard wind here two thousand years ago,
Over Ephesian homes and up their peopled streets.
I think as I hear these winds blowing strong today,
Maybe your conversations are lost upon these winds,
Words spoken on the crystal air in your great city.
Saint John, there are nostalgic winds in broken bones
Where this great city of the world once used to be,
In Asia Minor, where Christianity once thrived.
Saint John, why did we come here? Why do we return?
I read your *Revelation* when I was a boy,
I read your *Revelation* when I was a man—

This prophecy of God—and did not understand.
I read *Ephesians* too and here is Ephesus.

And here in Ephesus lived Christians and the Jews.
The Moslems were not born and Jewish faith was old.
And Christianity was in its first beginnings.
Among the bones of Ephesus the Christians grew.
Saint John, you've had and you still have, over this
        world,
Billions of followers, billions of faithful readers,
And writers of this world, Saint John, who will envy
        you
In your inspired portrayal of the word of God.
No wonder people from this earth are here today,
People of many tongues from places far away.
They come to Ephesus to see uncovered bones.
They came to your church, theater, and Great White
        Way,
And to the Old Agora strewn with fields of boulders.
These many stones were neatly hewn by human hands.

Saint John, you've walked the streets in Ephesus'
        agora,
There purchased food and clothes, items to sustain
        life.
The Jews were merchants then in Ephesus, as they
Are now in largest cities scattered over earth.
A few things do not change with centuries of time.

Ah, what a place was ancient Ephesus, its harbor
With ships from over all the known world sailing here
Into this harbor, trade ancient Ephesians knew.
Now, merchants, Jew, Gentile, and Christian
        dreamers gone;
All have gone back to dust except stone walls and
        streets.
These are remains enough to show what once was
        here.

A century hence all Ephesus will be uncovered,
In flatland by the harbor, high upon the hill.
And in the century to come one thing is certain:
There will be world visitors around your empty tomb,
And the wind,
                the wind,
                        the lonesome,
                                the Ephesian
                                Wind,

Will blow loudly,
            sadly,
                    sweetly,
                            strongly,
                                    never
                                        weakly
On Ephesus, this great world city's last remains,
Crying for something lost that will not come again.

You helped to bring us here, Saint John. Maybe this
    wind
Is whispering something to invisibles near us.
Speaking to little groups around your empty tomb
Where we are speaking Spanish, Greek, English,
    Turkish.
Our words are being carried away and mixed by wind.
This wind is good at mixing words in Ephesus.
Good-bye, apostle John; good-bye for now to you
And Ephesus but not good-bye forever.

DRY WIND OF EPHESUS

Dry wind of Ephesus
Naked, insensible,
If stones could write here
Each could write so many books
For you on Ephesus,
Too many books for Celsus'
Great Library to hold!

Mouth on, dry-throated wind,
Your words of destiny!
Blow your dry muted music
For them no longer here,
For them returned to dust;
Only the dream is left.

Your wind lips cannot speak;
They cannot shape a word.
Your tongue is dry and parched.
These holy men walk here
No more in Ephesus:
You will not find Saint John.
You will not find Saint Paul.
Somewhere invisible
They might brood over earth
And for their city lost,
Evasive to their dream.

Blow down the Marble Street,
Ephesians' Great White Way;

Blow over Trajan's Fountain,
Palace Municipality,
Theater and Old Agora,
And through Celsus' Library;
You will not find them here.

Dry wind, your tender skin
Is scratched by locust thorns
And blistered by the sun.
Still madly you search on,
The only moving thing
In Ephesus to search!
Never in any city
Have such men walked together,
To spread a living light,
To spread light for the world.

Lament, you dry-lipped wind!
Lament, you wordless wind,
Perpetual in your mumblings.
Lament for what has been
Back through the distant years;
Here withering grass and trees
Are begging for your tears.

There's nothing left here but a wind.

STRONG VOICES IN A BLOWING AUGUST
WIND

When Paul preached over there on Mars' Hill
He fashioned something for the centuries.
His was a message that has never died.
His was a message soon to be received
And in succeeding years spread over earth.
As I sit here upon another hill
Where I can look down on stone-barren Mars,
Up with wind strong enough to blow one down,
This hill made famous by great men who dreamed,
Who left a temple here against the sky,
The Parthenon world millions come to see,
It sits beneath a blue-domed Grecian sky.
Now, I sit on a stone where singing wind
Minutes ago tried hard to blow me down,
Sheltered by pine trees from an August sun,
Fiery enough to melt all waxen wings.
With thousands from world countries here to see
The Parthenon, Mars' Hill, earth's sacred stones,
I hear strong voices in this blowing wind.
Despite the many languages spoken here,
I hear the ancient voices from the past
Lamenting for new messages not here
And for return of beauty they created.
Hundreds climb up, discovering Mars' Hill.
Among the hundreds climbing freely there,
Who has a new message of hope to give
Our troubled world in this great hour of need?
Blow on, you troubled winds, so all may hear.

Blow on and never let their voices die,
Lamenting ancient voices from the past,
Old Socrates and Pericles and Paul,
Phidas, Ictinus and Callicrates,
Crying for what has been upon this earth,
Crying for what has never come again.

BLOW BACK, ATHENIAN WINDS

Books, coats, cameras, magazines in place,
Seat belts fastened, "no smoking" sign flashing,
Our four-motored plane rolled down the runway.
The pilot raced the motors before take-off.
The tall, handsome, black-eyed Greek stewardess
    smiled.
"Pressure will mount in a few minutes," she said.

"Here, have some chewing gum to ease the pressure."
And when the plane began to increase speed
Over the wet runway until airborne,
Beyond our little window we could see
Old Thessalonika's white stone buildings
Beside waves breaking on the Aegean Sea,
And high Acropolis, most scenic part
Of ancient Macedonia. I looked again,
Again before I said my last farewells.

Up, we arose and banked and circled; far
And on my right I saw Mount Olympus,
Home of the ancient gods. "Was Zeus up there?"
I wondered. "On snow-capped Mount Olympus?
And was there trouble there among the gods?"
Flying away from this god-home, Olympus,
I did not see the world of ancient gods.
Now we unfastened belts and leveled off,
But not for long, We fastened belts again.
Always this was the flight Greeks feared the most.
"I love you," Naomi said. She put her hand in mine.

"Yes, flying with you," she said, looking down
On jagged mountains and the rough terrain.
"And I love you. If we could live forever!
Love is a wonderful thing," I said, looking down
Into valleys inhabited once by gods.

"There is not time enough for love," she said.
"If we live long there won't be time enough."
Our big plane nosed into the volleying wind.
The wind is everywhere in Greece; in skies,
Down on the land, up valleys, and on shores.
Everywhere in Greece there's wind contact,
The gentle and strong winds that one must face.
On lonely nights there is the sound of wind
That cries and sings on land and over water,
And everywhere are everlasting sounds
Of sea, since its long fingers are extended
Into the shorelines. "I love you, love you!"

I hold Naomi's hand in mine as we sail on
Above this land where old love gods have dwelled
And in their jealousies they quarreled and fought.
And on we sailed into Athenian skies,
Above a warmer land with love and song.
Still hand in hand, we entered clouds that spiraled
Into white domes, higher than Mount Olympus.
Athenian winds have blown so many things
To all the world. We sailed through these god-skies

Above immortal Athens with stone shining,
Acropolis, world people came to see.

"Love is endurable and wonderful."
I hold Naomi's hand as our plane banks,
Circles the city twice, descends for landing.
Then we deplane into ancient Athenia,
Still holding hands, though years have passed for us
And youth has long been buried with the years.
I knew now how the ancient gods had felt
When they soared over their historic homeland,
Borne by the warm Athenian winds that still
Delight, excite, both gods and men in love.

IN DELOS BY THE SEA

Important Delos by the sea
Where Great Apollo first saw light,
Two hundred thousand once thrived here
In merriment, in beauty, laughter.
Where Great Apollo first saw light,
Ships came to Delos from all lands
To buy and sell prize merchandise.
Merchants grew rich on this god-island,
Land-dot on blue Aegean scroll.
Ships sailed into this perfect harbor
Where Delos by the sea rose up
The gentle slope to mountain top,
Mycenaean ruins where it began;
Up where Aegean winds came in
Like sheets of silver from the sea.
Moonlight and sunlight, Apollo
Sent, were gold and silver flames.
But who remembers now one name?
Rich merchants once lived here.
Their rock-walled homes, hotel for guests,
Deep cisterns and theater remain,
These traces excavat'd from the dust.
Stone lions gaunt and empty-eyed
Stand guard awaiting their return.
Gone with their God Apollo,
The winds and waters cry for them
In this immortal loneliness.

TO MYKONOS, OUR GREETINGS
AND FAREWELLS

Over your waving sea-bright waters
Your tender takes us from our ship,
Anchored, awaiting our return.
We greet you in your friendly city.
White houses, narrow streets, your people
Friendly. You welcome us ashore.
We visit shops. We buy from you.
We hear the sheep bells on your hills
Above waves lapping on your shores.
Three thousand island people on
Your fifty-three square miles of world
To hold your living and your dead;
Now and for countless centuries
Beneath a cloudless sky out here
Surrounded by the singing waters
Alone where winds are never still.
What do these old winds have to tell you?
White houses dot your gentle slopes.
Gardens and vineyards and your flocks
Give balance to your island world.
Your Mykonos, the beautiful!
Your fishermen come with their catch.
They let their nets dry in the sun.
We are no strangers here with you.
We greet, are greeted, love and are loved.
We spend a little time with you
And then we say, "Farewell." Return
Unto our anchored ship. We wave.

We wave to your white city when we sail.
We see you waving back to us,
You gathered on your lonely shore.
You and your Mykonos we may
Not see again, but love for you
And souvenirs we take away.
Fond memories of friendly people.
Good faces and your peaceful land.
Old winds and waters all around
Will live with us in hearts and minds,
In distant lands across the seas.

WHERE PINDAR LIVED

Leave the stones piled high where Pindar lived;
Each stone his eyes have seen, his hands have touched.
Stones that housed him are closer than the dust
Time has evaporated in a slow decay. . . .
Wind can blow dust but not the stones away.

Pindar could see in all directions here,
Waters from Theban springs that cured all ills,
Cotton and grain that grew on Theban plains,
In valleys and upon Boeotia's slopes!

In ancient Thebes among the tumbled stones,
Upon that plot of sacred space where Pindar lived,
Grass and the wind have secrets they can't tell;
The dandelions look up without surprise,
Reflecting sunlight in their golden eyes.

Pindar: spiritual unity of Greek Art.
Pindar: conservative who could not change
Whenever growing Greece changed in his time.
Four-and-twenty centuries have passed
Since Pindar walked these streets in ancient Thebes,
And centuries before, his ancestor,
God Cadmus, founded his immortal Thebes.

Time and not the torch tumbled this house
And it is definitely known Pindar lived here.
Where Pindar lived, the place is sacred now.
Things closest to him are the lichen'd stones,

The grass and dandelions, his yard-green earth
And old Boeotian winds that bend the grass.
These are the only durable things that last
While four-and-twenty centuries file past.

WHERE ANGRY WINDS BLOW SOFTLY

This is the season for the strong winds blowing,
Young, strong winds uninvited in Iran.
A stranger here myself, I feel their vigor
Over this ancient land the Persian knew,
In Persepolis, across dry wastes
Once called "breadbasket" of Persia.
They blow up dust around the fire temple
Where Cyrus bowed to worship.

And now they sing above his empty tomb.
How poetry is respected in Iran;
It's chanted by the farmers in the field,
Quoted by those who cannot read or write.
Yes, poetry is their culture to the bone.
They work through seasons when strong winds are
    blowing
High on this table-land above the world.

Winds carry thick black clouds that fade to blue
From tall industrial stacks in Teheran.
Round Isfahan's blue mosque these strong winds roar.
Here aspens' yellow leaves fight valiantly
Against the tyranny of angry winds
Which force them to depart their mother trees.

Why blow so angrily when I am here
To visit great Hafiz and Saadi's tombs
In beautiful Shiraz, "the poets' city,"
Which Persian poets gave to all the world?

Shiraz, the only place these angry winds
Blow softly, reverently for world renown;
Hafiz and Saadi sleeping in their tombs,
Elaborate mausoleums kings don't have
Through all the ages of all ancient lands.

KOREA TO THE WORLD

Koreans, tell us about yourselves!
Shout to the world about Korea!
Why imitate small Literatures,
Indefinite schools of thought?
Koreans, tell us about your culture,
Older than our America!

Tell us about your people's dancing,
Their dancing to the singing drums.
Describe for us your gay costumes,
Your land in winter when skates ring
On frozen rivers and rice paddies.
Tell us about your springtime land,
Green world a-glow with feathery blooms,
Your valleys, rivers, terraced lands.
Tell us about your wholesome laughter,
Trials, tribulations, songs of sorrow;
Sing bravely from your deep heart's core.

Tell us your love for education
And how you educate your people,
And how you hold your freedom won
And paid for dearly with your blood.
Freedom, common denominator
Of man, you hold at any price!
Stay proud, Koreans; rise and sing!

Koreans, you are durable,
A mighty northern race of man,

Improving unproductive land,
Building homes and factories,
Making a new place in the sun.

Winters and wars, we want to know,
And stories of your individuals.
You have not lived by food alone;
You have the spirit of a race.
Whence cometh your mighty strength?

Young writers imitate no one,
No country but your own Korea.
Strong in your bodies, be as strong
To sing Korea to the world!
We will rejoice to hear, Koreans,
Song from Korea's deep heart's core,
Your song of songs: *Korea to the world!*
Sing! Sing of your beloved Korea!

APRIL IN KENT

April in Scotland has an arctic chill.
Ask me, for I know mountain and the moor.
I lived in Scotland in wintry April,
But England has an April men adore.
One day I journeyed south the way birds went;
On wings and wheels I reached a springtime world,
No fairer land than the channel coast in Kent,
Where April's apple blossoms were unfurled
A lilting white cloud over fruitful land;
And here the gulls flew in their wind-sliced arcs
Above the cloud-bloom and the white-foam sand.
Kent was as springtime as a hundred parks,
A paradise until the month was over
Beneath an ever-changing English sky.
I followed roads from Cornwall back to Dover.
April in Kent once more before I die.

HORACE'S THEME

Go back to Poet Horace, if you will,
Chronicler substantial and the good
With poetry of valley and the hill.
Even winds blew for him in singing mood.
A Roman poet with his imperial dream,
Lifting his people up from decadence,
He chose the stalwart and the positive theme;
Back to the land and rural independence,
Back to the farm to grow and harvest grain,
Reviving games their ancestors once played,
Back hoeing plants, feeling sunshine and rain!
Can we believe the dreams this poet made,
Diminutive Horace, giant architect with words
That soothed his restless Romans, helped them find
Beauty all-Roman, even to stars and birds,
Bringing to them new life and peace of mind?

WHERE APRIL SINGS

In Cairo April whispers to the Nile,
A tired river nearing Journey's end;
April in Cairo all the stone gods smile
And reeds in reverence by the river bend.
April in Cairo has Pharaonic face
And brings a million out to Freedom's Square.
They come with laughter and they fill the place,
Moon over them and flower gardens there.
The Pyramids keep vigil on the sand;
They've seen five thousand Aprils come and part
From a jasmine and a lotus-scented land,
Where Egypt is an image in each heart.
Here snowy egrets fly on sacred wings
Above the silver Nile in clean bright air.
All Egypt is alive when April sings;
Soon I shall pack again and journey there.

The World
as Universal
Brotherhood

WORLD MUSIC

Stand here and listen to world music in
These spreading elm boughs with summer leaves,
Soft music notes for universal wind.
Here you will hear earth's finest symphonies.
Stand under leaves in wind in constant motion;
Hear music durable since time began
In summer's sweet recessional devotion.
Beneath these boughs interpret if you can
This unrecorded music from the spheres;
Feel flow of freshet wind against your face
And let your thoughts return to yesteryears
And billions who have known the wind's embrace;
To primitives who heard this music when
Young earth was first awakening from sleep,
Soft nature symphonies not penned by men
Still stirring from the universal deep.

EACH MAN IS KINGDOM,
EACH MAN IS DREAM

We are now springtime brothers in our world,
When once we lived a million miles apart.
Our small allegiance flags rose up unfurled;
Misunderstandings clouded mind and heart.
Our dream, world-over now: reunion, joys,
To make our new beginning April spring,
Extended living and no one destroys.
Billions of future young will rise to sing!
Each man is kingdom and each man is dream.
Earth has accepted all old dreamers' dust
With blowing wind and liquid in the stream.
All will tie with new dreams because they must,
For all old dreams must be the residue
From which we take the bloom, return the fruit.
Our world will be a dream so vastly new;
We take the beauty and return the loot.

THE DESTINY OF MAN

The destiny of man is big, my friend,
As high as walls of blowing wind are high;
And, as to depths, I know there is no end
Of mortal mansions born to live and die.
There is no end to love and joy and kiss,
No end to all the futile words we fling;
So little do we live, so much we miss,
So much of love and life and bitter sting.
Through soft eyes of the grass I can discern
Album of Destiny's fine photographs.
Worn out by years of living, they return
To wooing worms of earth and epitaphs.
The destiny of man within these pages
Is colored from rock-colors of the earth,
These lovers, fighters, drinkers, workers, sages .
Lovers of life, of hate, of joy and worth.

LET US BE BROTHERS

Let us be brothers to the elements,
Love lightning, storm, and growth in summer life;
Rich growth in warm soil coaxed by the elements,
From soothing rain to wind that wields a knife.
Let us be unafraid of what's to come
Out of the great earth we are living on;
The fifing wind, the heavy thunder drum,
And pitty-patty marching rain at dawn.
Let us be brothers to the land to live,
Set new young trees among old stumps and rocks.
Let us be neighbors, learn to take and give,
Back on our land be brothers to the fox;
Be brothers to the human-templed flesh
That has such little stay upon this earth!

TISSUE OF BUD AND BLOSSOM

In living clay, warm kisses we possess,
We who are tissues of blossom and bud.
Now far removed from earth's cool loveliness,
We are the lovers in wind-variant moods,
Reminded that that which we walked upon
Someday will hold our enriched resignations.
In our expectancy of brighter dawn
We will not kiss, nor will we stir emotions.
This urge to love resplendent in our dust
Now so alive and drinking air and sun,
We must accept; lips meet because they must
Until that time our blossoms come undone.
Can we remain reluctant in this hour?
Creative and beautiful, we are
Tissue of bud and blossom on the flower,
And each as individual as a star.

WILL DEATH BE FLYING
IN THE MORNING?

Will death be flying in the morning
Forever on to something new?
Flying when the dawn is breaking
And glorious sun begins to rise?
Flying over world awakening?
Crimson clouds like wildrose petals?
Canyons deep between cloud mountains?
No cup of coffee, but the eye,
To fathom what was never seen
Into this strange untravel'd land?
In death can I have motion in
And on forever and forever?

Tell me, who wants to sleep forever?
Forever bound in nothingness?
If death could mean an endless flight
When dawn is breaking and the sun
Is rising over words and new
Tomorrows where my phantom glides,
Then death would be eternal like
The flowing of a mighty river,
The blowing of a mighty wind!

Whatever this is that I have,
Motion forever that compels
Actions, funs, thoughts as many as
Bright mornings splendors from the sun,
I've found, and will hold if I can.

Surrender flesh, but still be I,
A human river flowing on
Through each new morning's rose-lipped dawn,
Forever through the Universe,
Forever new and endless space,
Exploring what I've never found
And seeing what I've never seen.

HOW CAN ONE SLEEP?

Restless is this night with a soft moon hanging
Red as a sliced beet under lichen stone;
Wind and the leaves are cymbals softly clanging
Music for him who loves to walk alone.
Night has no barrier for a man whose brain
Grows wild with her realms of poetic moods;
He feels and hears the wind and tastes the rain
When it drips from the leaves in poplar woods.
Night is godsend to man when it is full
Of darkness, mud, and blowing wind and cloud—
Night is a joyous mood that's beautiful;
Night is a whispering ghost in velvet shroud.
How can one sleep when wind and darkness stir?
How can one let his active brain be dead?
How can he lie awake night-long to hear
A million words of facts that should be said?

TIME'S IMMORTAL CLOCK

"Tick-tock, tick-tock," all through the long dark night.
"Tick-tock, tick-tock," says Time's immortal clock;
"I cannot pity man in his strange plight."
"Thrum thrum," Rain answers, beating on a rock;
"I've measured Time since wilderness began
And there was darkness on the mighty deep.
I've measured time before there was a man,
When all was void and all eternal sleep."
"What is this thing called Love?" Grass asks the Rain,
"And who are Sammie Raines and Etta Ash,
Whom I must resurrect to bloom again?"
"Do not ask me," Rain answers with a splash.
"They are immortal lovers," Wind explains
To Grass and Rain and Time. "They must not die.
I'll waft their story over hills and plains,
To every living thing in Earth and sky."

THERE IS NOT ONE OF US IMMUNE TO JOY

Stab at futility in anger, men,
April no less than April life forever.
Strike at futility and strike again;
Reach up toward inviting stars forever!
We are young kingdoms with our dreams that reach
Never beyond where hands can't grasp and hold;
New world of hope and peace we now beseech,
No exploitations, death and cankered gold!
Our flesh is dust; our human time is brief;
Our future has been warned by all the past.
Who stands before our dreams will come to grief;
The new world that we make is one to last.
There is not one of us who would destroy
World we hold out before us in our dream;
There is not one of us immune to joy,
Not one who will refuse to swim upstream!

FALL GENTLY, RAIN

The gentle April rain is chlorophyll.
Soft splinters fall to penetrate
Where resurrection is appearing late,
For life, cold-blooded, winter could not kill.
Fall gently, rain, to create sustenance
To feed a body that contains a life,
For sustenance is durable for strife.
Fall, rain; awaken life and stir romance.
Autumn to April is too long for sleeping,
Too long to close the eyes and rest the mind,
Too long to lose the light and miss the wind,
Too long for laughter from old autumn's weeping.
Fall gently, rain; let April's liquid given
Soak in life's sustenance so all can rise
Where earth's green canopy will soothe their eyes,
Rise to their dream of love in April heaven.

WE WENT TO CATCH A STAR

Proud youth of yesterday walked out with me;
With perfect nets we went to catch a star.
Each sought his star from vast eternity
But older people said we went too far.
Our elders said they tried in youthful spring
To no avail, applied their mind and heart
And from their sphere with nets they sought to bring
Unto their fellow man this precious art.
An elder cried: "Oh, where are we today?
The stars we tried to snare were out of reach!
But go, you young, go on your April way;
It takes a little span of years to teach!"
Where are the youth and I of yesterday?
Do not ask me where those proud ones have gone!
I've learned we must let springtime have its way,
Each seek his star before his youth is done!

COME HERE, YOU LIVING ONE

Come here, you living one; pick up this dust
And throw it to the wind and to the sun.
It has a certain pallor none can trust.
Though, too, it flies windward unto the sun.
What goes into the sun, in thin-air sheen,
I ask of you, you living girl in bloom?
Are you dust of some summer flower died green?
Or dust of any flower that died in bloom?
It is some pallor of soft-pallor-dust
That shines like amber from the sweet windflower
Only because Time's shortened seasons must
Crumble the petals and dry-rot the hour.
It is green Scorpion's dust before the sun,
The pallor of it likely to fool none.

THINGS THAT LAST

What facts are certain? Not even cities,
For yesterday they were built on a plain.
Today, of all their splendors, dusts remain.
And for the laughter there the wind hums ditties.
Facts are most uncertain, for even stone
Disintegrates into positive decay
And a breath of wind coud blow the dust away.
There is futility in everything.
And the thing most beautiful soonest goes—
Beauty of flesh, white fragrance of the rose,
The colored feathers on a rooster's wing.
And when we turn to look upon the past
We find few chosen words are things that last.

HERE IT IS

The earth is a gentle mother.
The leaves are her children.
The summer is the long warm day
when her children go to play.

The autumn is the evening.
She gently calls them in.
She blows her cold breath
into each little face
and they fall asleep
upon her bosom.

DO NOT FEAR AUTUMN DEATH

Do not fear autumn death; it is not certain,
No more than autumn wind that strangely whines
Is certain when you feel it shake the curtain
Of dead milkweeds and flute through trumpet vines.
Do not fear death, you who walk out this morning
With collars high to keep wind from your face.
The dead leaves fall with no or little warning,
And death is in the wind, is everyplace.
This is young autumn death, the beautiful dead;
And leaves mauve, yellow, gray, scarlet, and brown
Cling to late summer's sky above my head.
But at each gust of wind clouds shatter down
From death-clutched fingers from ribs where they
    cling.
If they just knew: through autumn death comes
    spring.

NEW WORK IN SECOND SPRING

Something in death of leaves does stir my blood,
Just think the world of living things that pass—
The summer green leaves in the pasture wood,
The red sweet-williams, ferns, and daisied grass.
Season for them is over when the frost
Falls on the meadow and the pasture hill.
Soon flowers, weeds, and pasture grass are lost
In a new world so cold and white and still.
Then, autumn death, I ask this thing of you:
"Why don't you let the living grow forever?
They'd live forever were it not for you;
In autumn death they cannot die forever!
"Friend Farmer, through this autumn death, will
    bring
New life, new hopes, new work in second spring."

I DID NOT PLAN THIS WINTER

I did not plan this winter for the dead.
I did not make this rain and send the snow.
I did not send each to his narrow bed
To lie forever with the dirt below;
Nothing that we can do about it, only
Accept our season minus cash and glory;
Though it is dark herein and time is lonely
We must take rooms in this repository.
If I had made the plan, life would not change
And go beneath this drab earth's crusty curtain,
Go on to what's invisible and strange,
Go on to something, certainly uncertain.
My plan would be to keep them on this sphere,
Weakling and strong, let them keep living here.

HOLD TO A LIVING DREAM

Hold to a living dream if you have one,
For dream is not akin to dirt and stone.
What is more precious here beneath the sun
Than human dream? This something that you own
Created by your heart and pulsing brain
At any hour, through death's throes of sleep,
Or when you wake and walk in white spring rain,
Or in your youth or when the late hours creep?
Remember, stones will crumble; dirt will loose
An avalanche of dream in tender spring
To bud and flower into a luscious fruit. . . .
Winter, this dream will not be anything.
Only your dream has value and can last,
This best your pulsing heart and brain did give
From your substantial or your shattered past
That flowered when you gave it breath to live.

BRAIN PASSIONS

Not wailing wind of autumn in the leaves
That haunts us as the blooming call of spring
When new life stirs to mating behind leaves
And birds in wind-space meet and mate and sing.
This is the life that haunts more than the wind
Of autumn; this is the time when life begins anew,
When white clouds go a sailing in the wind
And fresh sweet buttercups drip with the dew.
This is the life that hurts these sleeping so,
When flowers and youth and wine-green wind return
Beneath a warm spring sun in its sweet glow.
No need to say brain passions do return
Unto the living, and maybe the dead
That molder where dead flowers toss their head.

WE CANNOT ESCAPE

Sere old October and bright leaves swirl down
Where autumn has transformed the tree and flower.
Death's colors, mauve, golden, russet, and brown
Ride on night wind in this October hour.
Death stalks the fields, where everything is dead
Except the trees, and they have gone to sleep
And are stubble fields long harvested,
Above a night wind, and stars a vigil keep!
In other lands these same night winds are crying
And there is death on land and in the air,
For all the earth is either dead or dying
And we cannot escape death anywhere.
We can't escape until another spring
Brings back a resurrection to our earth
So life will bloom again, will rise and sing,
Will conquer death to give a clean new birth.

BE KIND TO DUST

Be kind to grains of dust that sting your face
For senseless winds have no thoughts of tomorrow;
Later they might deposit you someplace,
Yesterday's lips that kissed with joy and sorrow.

Remember, you are made of what you curse,
Those particles now getting in your eyes;
And getting in your mouth you think is worse,
Those little flecks of dust you so despise.

Who knows what brains and hearts these once have
      been?
And through what arteries these once have flowed?
Pumped by strong hearts of women and of men?
And by their love's emotions, paced and slowed?

Be kind to dust but curse the senseless wind
If foolishly you must waste your emotion;
Remember, living dust will in the end
Lose love and beauty, duty, and devotion.

AUTUMN AND THE ROSE

Lately, he has seen autumn in her cheek,
Nearly so beautiful as once the rose.
This hurts him deeply and he does not speak.
Thinking she'll go the way the blossom goes
He wonders why the rose too soon must die.
A flower most beautiful the soonest goes
No longer pointing its blooms to the sky,
To kiss with honey-fragrance wind that blows.
For her he thinks late autumn will come soon
Since in her cheeks the colors cease to thrive;
Colorless bloom beneath cool autumn's moon.
And he must be the stubborn oak alive.
He knows the autumn oak protects the rose.
The flower most beautiful the soonest goes.

IMPRESSION EIGHT

Now we arise on cold metallic wings
Behind the thrusting engines' mighty roar,
That lift us from the earth's cold winter floor.
Up, up to broad bright pavements of the wind;
We level off and fly toward the sun.
Below our darken'd world has not awaken'd;
He lies in stupor with sleep-blinded eyes.
We fly toward the new light that will wake him,
Bright morning light of new beginning day.
We fly toward the mighty morning sun
That planted sunset darkness yesterday.
Below us are the immoralities
Where Mammon reigns and crime pays dividends,
Where wrong is emphasized and right disdained.
Before us is the new clean morning light,
The new life-light to wake our sleeping world,
To cleanse and dress him in new robes of light.
For light is God and God is light and learning
And cleanliness is godliness admitted.
Darkness is ignorance; ignorance is evil.
We fly in fast pursuit, since time is late,
High over obstacles that hinder us,
The mountain, valley, river, rough terrain,
For we must seek this light that is God's light,
Light given only when we work for it.
We seek the new sunrise to change a world
That has grown Mammon-sick, -immoral, -evil!
We are in close pursuit and should we miss,
If there is time enough, we'll try again

No matter if wind-batter'd slopes be steep
In our ascent up to the higher level.
We can't be wrong in reaching for new light.
We can't be wrong to take this early flight,
To seek the morning sunrise where God is.

GO GATHER JOY

These young green winds of April will not die
Where youth behind closed walls breathe stuffy air.
Youth hear in their closed cells young April's cry
Over a world with springtime love out there.
Green winds tell them of paths for them to take
By rivers where waters are having fun,
In valleys where wildflowers are awake
With satin petals laughing at the sun.
Green winds tell April youth where they belong
Out in clean freedom of the earth and skies,
Where they can hear cold wind-and-water song,
Where they can breathe clean wind and exercise.
Awaken youth; now is the time or never.
Go after wine-green April life to hold.
Go gather joy to be with you forever,
Even to help you when you're growing old!

WING-BEATS

Have you not heard the words so many speak,
Whose flesh is brittle and whose brains are dumb,
Who lie in cells where not a word can leak
Up to soft cottony winds that hum?
Then how can you dispute the destiny
That comes to me, to you, and to our dead?
You can't, no more than say this is no tree,
When in *Album of Destiny* you read
The words of those who left our little throng,
Those gone that certain path that you must walk.
They came like you and sang their little song,
Stood on a stump and gave their little talk.
And now I ask of you, what are their words,
More than the wing-beats of a thousand birds?

LET US ARISE

Amidst the elements let us arise
Like lightning streaks of elemental fire,
And with the blood and thunder in our eyes
Tramp thorn-infested paths of our desire.
Your womb will surely stay the living flesh
Of stalwart sons and daughters yet unborn.
Clean hearts, fine blood, will yet replenish earth
And go afield by streaks of dawn at morn.
They'll know the earth as we, their sires, have known it.
They'll feel the earth as we, their sires, have felt it.
They'll have a love for earth and things upon it
And stubbornly hold earth as we have held it.
Let us breed better blood to carry on,
Than old blood which too often comes undone.

THE POET AND TOMORROW

A poet can't unite with other minds;
His is an only path to walk alone.
His thoughts like surging rivers, blowing winds,
He hears and understands a voice from stone.
A poet must escape the petty clan,
Evade the schools of blowing winds of thought.
Behind his poem there must be the man
Himself, sure of the artifice he's wrought
And proud he reached alone up for the stars
Despite his knowing he could not reach them,
Contented that he put dream above his cares
And that he puts his lifetime in his dream.
Unborn will know after his years have flown,
When poets of his time are taking sleep,
Whether he'll be among tomorrow's known,
When he will not be here to laugh and weep.

BOY BESIDE THE TRACKS

White mountains of soft curling smoke,
   Ascending to the sky
Above the lonesome railroad tracks
   As the passenger train zooms by.

Strange faces pressed against the panes,
   Eyes searching fail to see
A lonely boy beside the tracks,
   Envying their destiny.

INTERCESSION

How great thou art, dear God, how great thou art!
Obliterate the walls that separate,
Those in our mind and in our stubborn heart.
How nice to substitute your love for hate.
Your children have gone mad in their behavior
For termites penetrate the Christian Cross.
They don't believe mankind has any Savior
Except the politician and the labor boss.
How can your children stand for such a thing,
To substitute the stomach for the soul,
To have a politician, labor boss, for king
And Heaven be a fairy land of dole?
So great thou art, dear God; you surely see
Our need for you this hour to intervene,
To give us calm and practicality,
To take hate from our hearts and put love in.
Since thou art great, dear God, do intercede;
We need your guiding hand and one to lead.

HEAVEN'S GATE

On sunlit wings near Heaven's Gate we glide
Above this fluffy Elysian snow-cloud floor;
Up here where there is neither time nor tide,
The greatest sounds our trusty engines' roar.
Up here is space,
             clean wind,
                         blue sky and sun;
Up here is cleanliness above reproach.
Up here a future world has new begun.
Armies of conquest here will never march.
How beautiful above the depths of sky
Where stacked cloud-mountains reach for sun and
    star;
Here where strong currents of the space winds cry,
If there were only stations where we are!
These wings that carry us must soon descend
From Heaven's Gate to earth, our journey's end.

DREAM DOERS

Those who have been defeated and seek rest
Recount the splendor of their sundown past
In idle dream believing this is best.
They are regretful their lives will not last.
Their past is flame the future could not hold
Of multimillion dreams they hoped would pass
To peaceful earth where rainbows would unfold
On their thought-meadows of the lusher grass.
They did not know the germinating seed
Would work to pollinate the rose and thorn,
To give unto our earth a woeful need,
To make embattled night a sunlit morn.
Dream doers know the last is with them now,
When they must never let the dream escape,
By watching those defeated youth learn how
In their young years to forge good dreams in shape.

APRIL'S A SONG

April is spring, a chit-chit chatty spring
When leaf and bud and bloom all chime together.
Chit-chat, tra-la, tra-la; they chime together!
April is many a multicolored wing;
April chit-chat is many a sing-sing-sing,
A sing-chit-chat with a heart light as a feather!
April, wind-colored-green, is a get-together;
April is a tra-la-la and a sing-sing-sing!
April's a month of two's on wings and feet,
Tra-la, tra-la, tra-la, a groom and bride,
Entwined, love-vined, beside, beside, beside.
April's a song when life is young and sweet.
Tra-la, tra-la, chit-chat, chit-chat, sing-sing!
Tra-la, young April wears no yes-me-do;
Young April is the time to bill and coo,
A time for bill and lip and air-thin wing!

MUSIC WASTED ON THE WIND

Attune your doubtful ear to earth;
The snake has rhythms in his crawl,
Sweet melodies of slyness, mirth;
No voice, his song is eternal.

After his resurrection of
Winter's hibernation sleep
Over soft grass he sings of love
And a lover's tryst that he will keep.

His singing may not be your choice
From one mankind considers nil;
Without a voice he has a voice
And destiny he must fulfill.

He writes an autumn symphony
Over dead leaves to his abode,
To sleep in his eternity,
To dream of rabbit and the toad.

It's time he must divest his art
And leave his symphonies behind;
Each season he has played a part
With music wasted on the wind.

ANCIENT SONG

It seemed
  to me
that God
  was an ancient song
    among the minds
      of many people,
and that he
  was passing
    deathward
      mournfully.

THE WIND AND STARS

The wind and stars are not substantial food.
There's something in their substance of deceit.
The wind will whet an appetite for mood;
The star's a toy that lures you after it.
Walk in the wind and meet it face to face
And hear it whisper magic to your ears,
And in one moment there is not a trace
That it has come and left your eyes in tears.
On winter night you climb a frozen hill
And stand upon the highest jut of stone;
You'll find a sky of stars is higher still,
And you will stand beneath them all alone.
All you can do is write a song for them
With moods of unsubstantial wind within it;
Know wind and stars are both a fragile dream
That lives with you through every fragile minute.

THIS DUMB MOAN MUSIC

Drip—drip, drop—drop; drip—drip; sush—sush;
    sigh—sigh!
Drip—drip, drop—drop; drip—drip; sush—sush;
    sigh—sigh!
That is this dumb moan music of the world.
Drip—drip, drop—drop; drip—drip; sush-sush;
    sigh-sigh!
Drip—drip, drop—drop; drip—drip; sush-sush;
    sigh-sigh!
The falling of rose petals now frost-curled!
Sish—sish, sigh—sigh; oo -oooooo—oo; sish-sish;
    sigh—sigh!
Sish—sish, sigh—sigh; oo -oooooo—oo; sish-sish;
    sigh—sigh!
This dumb moan music blowing down the world!
Tish—tish; tip—tip; top—top; tip—tip, tish—tish!
Tish—tish; tip—tip; top—top; tip—tip, tish—tish!
Cool autumn rain with winter setting in!
Gods on night wind, why can't you hear my crying?
The clutch of power fingers cuts the wind
Of my blood kin who are so slowly dying!

SOUGHT-AFTER PARADISE

Lie on the grass and feel wind over me,
Lifting my hair, soothing my sleepy eyes;
If this could be sought-after paradise!
What is more joyous than the feel of wind
That gently shakes the snowy dogwood petals?
This energetic wind that soothes the skin?
This young spring wind that dominates our Aprils?
Young April wind can dominate without us,
With touch and sound and energetic stir.
Like leaves on trees we hang as tremulous;
We are in separation from this sphere.
Our seasons are like flowers and leaves and grass,
A season far too short to reach love's height.
We're like young April's timely winds that pass
Into the shadow of the coming night.

ACROSS THE EMPTY FIELDS

Across the empty fields Winter retreats,
Releasing his high mortgage on the weather—
Then wary Spring trips back on airy feet
And buds and grass and wind all laugh together:
"Where is the mortgage Winter held on weather—
Where is the Winter, desolate and gray?
Gone—gone—and gone, we hope, forever."
The wind-flowers nod: "Yes, gone forever,
And gone we hope forever and a day—"
And that is all the white wind-flowers said,
Standing by last year's stems so cold and dead.
The land is left a scroll for winds to read—
The gray-starved land is used to birth and growth.
The gray-starved land is left to Spring and youth.

AVALANCHE TO LOVE

Why resurrection in an April spring
And stirring times when nations fall apart?
Why dedication of the mind and heart?
How truthful is the knowledge we impart?

Down in the nether world where no birds sing
There is no light to show a handsome face.
There is no strength in arms for strong embrace.
There are no sparks to propagate our race.

April has come as avalanche to love,
Young love, spring love, their elders can't approve;
For like spring winds spring love is on the move,
Young April love the world cannot reprove.

Beneath the blossoms on the wind-blown tree
Young arms have strength and there is liberty,
When lips meet lips in our perpetuity,
Our Paradise where sap and blood run free.

RETURN

Young April's body is too manifest,
But April's beauty is no higher than
A kingdom of our living dust called man,
But with less savagery in her clay breast.
The lightning stab, rain-spike, and thunder-jar
Have not potentials of the bomb and gun.
With effort our aggrandizement is won.
April returns each year to where we are
And shines among the seasons and returns,
An answer of the flesh and blood and bone,
The blossom, bird and leaf and lichen stone.
Her lamps for nights and days: moons, stars, and suns.
April brings her glad tidings to the earth
To overcome the decadence and strife,
For April comes to bring us youth and life
And resurrection to imprison death.

Acknowledgments

"Beginning" reprinted by permission of *Esquire Magazine*. Copyright © 1956 by Esquire, Inc. "Rededication" reprinted by permission of *The Lyric*. Copyright © 1967. "Night Song" reprinted by permission of Ball State University *Forum*. Copyright © 1960. "The Two Houses" reprinted by permission of *The Lyric*. Copyright © 1957. "Stay While April Is My Lover" reprinted by permission of *The Angels*. Copyright © 1967. "By the Bend in the Road" reprinted by permission of *Poem*. Copyright © 1967. "My Loves Will Remain When I Have Passed" originally appeared in *Harvest of Youth* published by The Scroll Press. "A Sincere Song" reprinted by permission of *New Letters*, successor to *The University of Kansas City Review*. Copyright © 1958. "Green River" reprinted by permission of *American Forests*. Copyright © 1957. "Joyously to Drift and Dream" originally appeared in *Educational Forum*, XXIII (1959), 406. "Spirit Growth" reprinted by permission of *Chicago Tribune Magazine*. Copyright © 1968.

"Shinglemill Symphony" reprinted by permission of *American Forests*. Copyright © 1965. "Oh What a Poem I Am In" from *Via Kentucky Highways*. Copyright © 1970. "Morning Interview" originally appeared in *Hawk and Whippoorwill*. Reprinted by permission of Estate of August Derleth. Copyright © 1961. "Railroad Sounds" originally appeared in *Harvest of Youth* published by The Scroll Press. "The Flower Gatherer" reprinted by permission of *Ladies' Home Journal*. Copyright 1949 by Downe Pub., Inc. "April Is Life" reprinted by permission of *The Angels*. Copyright © 1968. "To Be Just One of Them" reprinted by permission of *The Angels*. Copyright © 1968. "Prolific Dirt" reprinted by permission of *Esquire Magazine*. Copyright © 1955 by Esquire, Inc. "Active Summer Moves Too Fast" reprinted by permission of *Laurel Review*. Copyright © 1970. "The Heart Flies Home" reprinted by permission of *Ladies' Home Journal*. Copyright © 1958 by Downe Pub., Inc. "Send Me a Memento" reprinted by permission of *Approaches*. Copyright © 1967.

"To Be a Poet" reprinted by permission of *Pegasus*, published by the Kentucky State Poetry Society, Fall 1971. "I Never Tried to Write a Book" from *Man with a Bull-Tongue Plow* by Jesse Stuart. Copyright 1934 by E. P. Dutton & Co. New, revised edition copyright © 1959 by Jesse Stuart. Reprinted by permission of the publishers, E. P. Dutton & Co., Inc. "Their Eyes Have Seen" reprinted by permission of *Esquire Magazine*. Copyright © 1956 by Esquire, Inc. "Too Soon, Too Early" reprinted by permission of *Poem*. Copyright © 1967. "Enchanted April" reprinted by permission from *The Colorado Quarterly* V (Spring 1957). Copyright © 1957 by the University of Colorado, Boulder, Colorado. "Resurrection Reasoning" reprinted by permission of *The Angels*. Copyright © 1968. "Eye of the April Sun" reprinted by permission of *American Forests*. Copyright © 1967. "Hold April" reprinted by permission of *The Lyric*. Copyright © 1956. "Songs That Sing Themselves" reprinted by permission of *New Letters*, successor to *The University of Kansas City Review*. Copyright © 1957. "In the Music of the Wind" originally appeared in *Poems from the Hills*, ed. William Plumley, published by Morris Harvey College Publications, 1971, 1972. "Mae Marberry" from *Man with a Bull-Tongue Plow* by Jesse Stuart. Copyright 1934 by E. P. Dutton & Co. New, revised edition copyright © 1959 by Jesse Stuart. Reprinted by permission of the publishers, E. P. Dutton & Co., Inc. "I Know a Place" from *Man with a Bull-Tongue Plow* by Jesse Stuart. Copyright 1934 by E. P. Dutton

Index of Titles

About the Author and the Editor

Jesse Stuart is firmly wedded—not only to Naomi Deane Stuart, but to his 1,000-acre corner of heaven on earth in eastern Kentucky. It is an area of rare tranquillity encompassing pastureland, timber, creeks, an abundance of small wildlife. The noises of what we call civilization are notably absent. The occasional cough of a tractor sputtering to life half a mile away is largely blanketed by bird songs and the nattering of mother raccoons scolding their young for misbehavior. Much of Stuart's best poetry and prose has stemmed from these same hills and valleys, but he has always been a traveler, both in body and spirit. The extraordinarily wide range of people, places and things evident in this collection of poems may surprise those who have tagged Jesse Stuart with the label "regionalist."

J. R. LeMaster, a Ph.D. from Bowling Green State University, was born in southern Ohio, and is now Chairman of the English Department at Defiance College. He is himself a poet and the author of two published collections, *The Heart Is a Gypsy* and *Children of Adam*. He has for several years studied Jesse Stuart's work closely, has published critical appraisals of it in a number of reviews and quarterlies, and is so close a follower of his work that Stuart was the subject of Dr. LeMaster's Ph.D. thesis. Married and the father of three children, he lives in Defiance, Ohio.